# CHRISTIE'S

*Review of the Season 1995*

# CHRISTIE'S

## *Review of the Season 1995*

Edited by

FRANCIS RUSSELL

Assisted by

JAMES PEILL

# CHRISTIE'S

Copyright © Christie, Manson & Woods Ltd., 1995

A CIP catalogue record for this book is available from the
British Library.

ISBN 0 903432 46 3

Printed by Watmoughs, Bradford and London

*Frontispiece:*
LEONARDO DA VINCI (Italian, 1452-1519)
Autograph manuscript, titled (on an additional eighteenth-
century manuscript title-page): 'Delle Natura, Peso, e Moto delle
Acque', consisting of scientific notes and observations,
later known as Codex Leicester and Codex Hammer
(Folio 16B:21 *recto* illustrated)
72 pages (36 leaves on 18 double sheets),
average page size 11¾ x 8⅞ in. (29.9 x 22.5 cm.), written
*alla mancina* (from right to left), in lines of varying length,
interspersed with approximately 360 illustrative drawings and
diagrams by Leonardo
Sold by the Armand Hammer Museum of Art and Cultural Center,
Los Angeles, California.
New York, 11 November 1994, $30,802,500 (19,405,575)
Record auction price for a manuscript

Leonardo's notes on this page encompass, in four parts, several
aspects of the theory and practice of dam building and flood control.
This manuscript is discussed in an article by Stephen C. Massey
and Hope Mayo on pp. 202-3.

**All prices include the buyer's premium where applicable.
The currency equivalents given throughout the book are
based on the rate of exchange ruling at the time of sale.**

# CONTENTS

# FOREWORD

## by Sir Anthony Tennant

When you look through the scholarly articles and illustrations in this *Christie's Review of the Season* you may, as I am, be struck anew by the variety as well as the value of the works of art we offer in our auction rooms in Europe, America and Asia during the course of the year.

We were fortunate this year to be entrusted with some exceptional things. The Leonardo da Vinci *Codex Hammer* for instance, is an illustrated manuscript of great importance to the history of our culture, illuminating as it does some of the complex speculations in the field of science and technology of one of the greatest geniuses of Western thought. The Codex fetched $30.8 million at Christie's New York, the highest price paid at auction during the year.

In Geneva a work of art of a very different kind, the crystalline Winter Imperial Egg by the master jeweller Carl Fabergé achieved the highest price yet seen for a work by Fabergé at S.Fr.7.26 million. It was originally commissioned by the last Czar in 1913 as an Easter present for his mother, the Dowager Empress Feodorovna, and thus is not only an exquisite example of the work of Fabergé, but also a poignant souvenir of a vanished dynasty.

An English masterpiece of exceptional quality, the *Portrait of the Royal Tiger* by George Stubbs, was one of the most important British pictures to come on the market for many years and was sold on behalf of the Trustees of the Portman family. It achieved £3.2 million, a record price for the artist at auction.

I am pleased to be able to report that Christie's Impressionist and Modern sales were successful both in London and New York. We were fortunate to be able to offer some outstanding pictures, of a higher quality than has been seen for some time. The first indication of a renewed confidence in these markets came when Toulouse-Lautrec's *Danseuse ajustant son Maillot (Le premier Maillot)* doubled its pre-sale estimate to sell for $4.8 million, and Warhol's *Shot Red Marilyn* sold for $3.6 million. In May, Important Modern Works of Art from the collection formed with a sure eye over many years by Mr. and Mrs. Ralph F. Colin made $34.4 million. I saw the Colin pictures in their Park Avenue apartment and I shall never forget the lovely *Nu assis au Collier* of 1917 by Modigliani which the Colins hung in their drawing room. It established a new record for the artist of $12.4 million. Nine paintings from this collection sold for more than $1 million.

In London an exceptionally good Monet of Rouen Cathedral sold for £7.6 million and an early Miro belonging to Gustav Zumsteg made £4.7 million. We sold over 90% by value of the pictures in our June Contemporary sale. Particularly notable were Yves Klein's *La Grande Bataille*, a Francis Bacon study and a seascape by Anselm Kiefer which established a new record for the artist at £485,500.

The market for Latin American paintings is also strong. In November Diego Rivera's *Vendedora de Alcatraces* sold for $1.1 million in New York, a record for a watercolour by any Latin American artist. It featured in a series of Latin American sales which totalled over $16 million, the highest yet achieved in this category by Christie's.

'Theme' sales, such as the now well-established 'Bird' sales, have been developed by Christie's to present pictures within a certain very specific area of interest, thus focusing international attention to previously under-developed areas of collecting.

In London the second Christie's sale devoted to the work of nineteenth and twentieth-century German and Austrian artists was an outstanding success. Christie's have taken the lead in recognizing the significance of these hitherto underrated schools and establishing their importance in the development of modern European art. The nineteenth-century section of the sale included *Fischerboot zwischen Findlingen am Ostseestrand* by Caspar David Friedrich, the great German Romantic artist, which realised £639,500. The top price in the modern section was for Karl Schmidt-Rottlluff's *Einfahrt* which made a record price of £958,500. It is a particularly fine example of German Expressionism.

'Interiors' a sale in London devoted to views of interiors through the ages, attracted interest from buyers all over the world; as did a previously unknown collection of watercolours for John Gould's celebrated *The Birds of Great Britain* which realised over £1 million. The display of these beforehand was described by *The Observer* newspaper as 'one of the best exhibitions in the country'.

The inaugural 'Visions of India' sale in London established Indian pictures, prints, drawings and photographs, together with the work of British artists who depicted India under the Raj, as a major new area of collecting, and five world record prices were set in the sale devoted to the Orientalists, European and American artists who drew inspiration from the Middle East and North America in the last century.

In a pioneering mood in New York the spectacular sale of the Dr. and Mrs. George S. Bayoud collection of works by Thomas Molesworth, consisting of extravagant Western furnishings from the Old Lodge in Glenwood Springs, Colorado was the highlight of Christie's 'American West Week' in June. The prices achieved tripled the estimates to total $2.9 million with 100% sold.

1994 has seen several other new initiatives by Christie's including a very successful inaugural sale in Israel of nineteenth and twentieth - century pictures. Good prices were paid for internationally known artists, particularly for the work of Marc Chagall, and for modern Israeli artists, such as Arieh Aroch and Avigdor Arikha.

Another Christie's initiative, this time in New York in April, was the inaugural New York Zachys-Christie's auction of Fine and Rare wines which attracted more than five hundred wine enthusiasts to Christie's Park Avenue. The sale lasted for nine hours and totalled $1.8 million – the largest sum ever realised for a wine sale in the United States.

In my opinion the most fascinating of all the consignments entrusted to Christie's over the past year have been single-owner collections, offering as they do, not only highly interesting provenance, but also the opportunity to see the diversity within collections formed by individuals of great taste and discernment whose choices form an intrinsic part of the history of taste and collecting.

The sale of works of art from Houghton created much excitement. It was, perhaps, the sale of the year. The viewing and parties were attended by about fifteen thousand people in New York, Paris, Seoul and London. In addition to the five hundred and forty people who attended the King Street sale, we took bids from over thirty telephone lines. The climax of the sale, the final lot, was *La Lecture de Molière* by Jean-François de Troy. It became the most expensive eighteenth-century French picture ever sold at auction, realising £3.9 million. Preparatory work for the Houghton sale had started in earnest five months beforehand. *The Spectator* commented of the catalogue that it was 'the greatest auction catalogue of the second half of the 20th century'. The magnificent William Kent and eighteenth-century French furniture looked stunning in an imaginative evocation of some of their original settings. This was Christie's at its best.

In New York, the sales of Old Master paintings, nineteenth-century paintings, sculpture, furniture, antiquities and jewels from the collection of Alice Tully, the noted American philanthropist and patron of the arts, offered a glimpse of the purest and most cultivated American taste of the twentieth century. I was lucky enough to see Alice Tully's beautiful things in her New York apartment overlooking Central Park.

Every single lot in the sale of Chinese works of art from the Arthur M. Sackler collections was sold in New York in December. Another fine collection, formed by Mr. and Mrs. Eddy Nicholson, perhaps the most important private collection of American furniture ever to come to the market, fetched $13.6 million in January.

Very different was the eclectic and highly personal collection of Rudolf Nureyev, which achieved nearly $8 million, double the estimate. We created room settings in Christie's Park Avenue which gave a glimpse of the extraordinary private world of this great dancer. There were queues stretching around the block.

1994 was an outstanding year on both sides of the Atlantic for furniture and works of art sold at Christie's and I believe has again emphasised our leadership of this market.

Jewellery has also done very well, being 28% ahead of the previous year. Three single-owner collections stood out; the sale of Vera Hue-Williams' jewels in Geneva in May was the highlight of the auction week. Her magnificent ruby and diamond necklace achieved $1,065,000. Jewellery from the collection of Alice Tully was 100% sold in New York at $2.1 million and Antique and Period jewellery from the collection of Mr. and Mrs. Ralph F. Colin was also 100% sold, reflecting a revival of interest in earlier and historical jewellery design.

Christie's has always been known for its expertise in the rarefied field of coloured diamonds. In November, a record of S.Fr.9.6 million was achieved for a pink diamond, and in the sale of magnificent jewels in April in New York, a flawless blue diamond realised $7.5 million, at $550,000 per carat the highest price per carat ever paid for a blue diamond at auction. In all, the three days of jewellery sales in New York in April yielded a total of $37.1 million, the highest total for jewellery sales in the spring/summer season in New York.

In Asia Christie's has successfully extended its sales of Western jewellery to Taipei and Hong Kong, in addition to launching the first-ever sale entirely devoted to jadeite (gem quality jade). This extremely successful sale which made over H.K.$74 million saw the Mdivani necklace, once the property of Barbara Hutton, sell for H.K.$33 million, the highest price yet paid for jadeite.

House sales which, since James Christie's earliest days have played such an important part in the history of Christie's, also did well. The auction of the contents of Keir offered effects from one of Scotland's oldest families in a very successful three day sale. Our King Street rooms saw the sale of furniture belonging to the late Dallas Pratt which achieved £1.1 million, and the sale of furniture, pictures and silver from Tythrop Park, also at King Street, achieved £496,500 for a pair of late George II mahogany dining room urns and pedestals in a sale which totalled £3.5 million, underlining once again the value of objects of good quality and excellent provenance.

This season has seen a further growth in business at Christie's South Kensington. Several new sale categories were introduced, including the first Jazz auction which realised a world record price of £93,500 for Charlie Parker's saxophone. The picture department held their first ever wildlife art sale and an inaugural sale of vintage film posters in March this year was timed to coincide with the celebrations marking one hundred years of cinema. The sale covered every genre of film and realised almost £300,000.

Rarities which will never come under one of our auctioneer's hammers drew ten thousand visitors to a major exhibition, *Foundations for the Future*, in January. Drawn from the collections of the University of Cambridge, the exhibition formed part of the University's fund raising campaign to continue its contribution to science and scholarship. Among the highlights of the historic exhibits was the Canterbury Gospels. This is thought to be among the books which Pope Gregory the Great gave to Saint Augustine to aid his mission to introduce Christianity to the English. Prior to this exhibition it had left Cambridge only for the coronation of Archbishops of Canterbury.

The astonishing diversity of works of art handled by Christie's 95 offices in 35 countries is a true mirror of the ebb and flow of the international art market and the currents and eddies in contemporary taste. No day at Christie's can ever be like any other, for there is almost always something beautiful, something curious, something of historical interest to be found in our salerooms, or to be seen in our many touring exhibitions.

There is also the excitement of the results of our original research, discoveries which add to our knowledge of the past, provenances augmented, works of art hitherto 'circle of' given scholarly attribution by our experts who are, together with our auctioneers, the very heart of our business. For the essence of Christie's is the combination of scholarship and salesmanship which brings so much interest and excitement to our auction rooms over the course of a year.

# SALES TO THE NATION

## by Edward Manisty

In reviewing the activities of Christie's Heritage and Taxation Department over the past season I realise how fortunate I am to be involved in sales of works of art to the Nation. For this is an exercise that can give satisfaction to many, involving as it does more than the mere transfer of artefacts from one owner to another. Such transactions can afford real benefits to Christie's clients, both tangibly, in reduced exposure to taxation on the disposal, and more intangibly, in that a well loved object passes to a new home where it will continue to be cared for and also become available for appreciation by a wider audience. The benefit to the public and the museums that serve the public is self evident. However, the satisfaction of my colleagues as experts in their fields of study is perhaps less so: their pleasure in seeing works of art acquired by public museums is very real. Finally, there is the satisfaction that I, and those who work with me in the Department, obtain in surmounting the obstacles that often arise in completing such transactions.

Indeed the path to success is hardly a bed of roses. Over the year, public museums have suffered further cuts in their grants from central Government. The National Heritage Memorial Fund, grappling as it is with the novel demands of administering a share of Lottery monies currently running at a rate in excess of £250,000,000 a year is still feeling its way towards deciding how it will respond to requests for grants for new acquisitions from a much wider spectrum of museum applicants. The administration of the other vital route for our museums to make new acquisitions – the offer in lieu of tax arrangement – remains as unuser friendly as ever. Nonetheless, there is real cause for optimism. The advent of Lottery funds will surely before long assuage, if not actually reverse, the outflow of important works of art from this country that has taken place over the last hundred years. There are signs that those who play a major role in defending the corner of our museums, led by the Reviewing Committee on the Export of Works of Art, are aware of the need to rally round the offer *in lieu* scheme and to see its administration improved.

A number of important archives have been acquired by the Nation through Christie's over the past twelve months. These have ranged from relatively small collections to the major acquisition by the British Library of the papers of the diarist John Evelyn, a transaction more fully explored elsewhere by Felix de Marez Oyens (pp. 194-5). Among smaller collections were the papers of the centenarian General Sir George Higginson (1826-1926) including his own account of the Crimean Campaign, and those of his father and uncle, who both served with the Grenadier Guards, of the Peninsular War, sold by private treaty to the Guards Museum. By way of contrast, the Osborn Muniments, a collection of deeds and estate papers relating primarily to the Manor of Chicksands in Bedfordshire, passes to the Bedfordshire County Record Office. In his *History of England*, Sir Keith Feiling declared 'the deepest influence upon a nation' to be 'the way in which its land is held', a thesis developed by Sir John Habbakuk in his recent magisterial study of English

landownership between 1650 and 1950, *Marriage, Debt and the Estates System.* The preservation of and availability to scholars of papers such as the Osborn Muniments constitute the foundation of such important studies.

The British Library Oriental & India Office Collections was the recipient of a collection of early nineteenth-century drawings and watercolours of Indian and Chinese interest recently rediscovered at Mount Stuart. From the collection of the 1st Marquess of Hastings, the albums comprise watercolours, notably by the Indian artist, Sita Ram, illustrating the travels of the Marquess, his wife and young children in India when he was Governor-General of Bengal, between 1813 and 1823. These superb albums complement the written journals kept by the Marquess and were designed to serve as a record for the future instruction of his children, who were perhaps too young to appreciate much of what they saw during their travels in India. Certainly the charming nature of many of the illustrations may be appreciated by both young and old.

An important addition to the British Museum's collection of Old Master drawings was secured with the sale by private treaty of Marco Zoppo's *The Dead Christ* and *Saint James Blessing the Roman Soldier*. It is considered to be one of the artist's earliest works, executed around 1455-57, and shows the intense enthusiasm for the Antique that his tutor Squarcione generated in those he taught. The work is closely related to drawings by Mantegna, another of Squarcione's pupils, and in particular to his now destroyed fresco in the Eremitani at Padua. The British Museum previously had nothing directly similar in type and function to this finished, double-sided sheet on vellum, which was probably intended for use as a private devotional object.

The National Portrait Gallery acquired two portrait miniatures of Thomas Cromwell by Hans Holbein the Younger. The two pictures, framed back to back in a circular gold locket, are of different dates: the earlier seems to be of the same date (around 1532) as Holbein's portrait of Cromwell in the Frick Collection, New York. The second, perhaps executed five or six years later, is similar, but varied to record the ageing of the subject over the intervening period. In this, he wears the chain of the Order of the Garter. Cromwell had risen to great influence under Henry VIII, becoming Lord Privy Seal and Lord Great Chamberlain. His fall from favour was sudden; honoured with the Earldom of Essex in April 1540, he was executed less than three months later.

Moving from the sixteenth to the twentieth century, Francis Bacon's *Study for a Portrait, March 1991* was added to the collection of the Scottish National Gallery of Modern Art in Edinburgh, it being the first work by the artist acquired by the Gallery. This important painting remaining in the artist's studio at his death, was ceded to the Nation by way of offer *in lieu*. This transaction provides a reminder that negotiated sales may be as relevant to artefacts created in the recent past as to those executed in earlier decades.

SITA RAM (active c.1810-20)
Lord Moira's European Servants in travelling Equipage
watercolour
Sold by private treaty to the British Library, London

FRANCIS BACON (British, 1909-1992)
Study for a Portrait, March 1991
oil and pastel on canvas
78 x 58 in. (198 x 147.5 cm.) Accepted *in lieu* of tax by
H.M. Treasury and allocated to the Scottish National Gallery of
Modern Art, Edinburgh

It is perhaps worth stressing that Christie's involvement in such sales is by no means limited to archives and paintings or to dealings with national museums. Notably, Christie's was instrumental in the acquisition by the Birmingham Museums & Art Gallery of busts of Matthew Boulton (1728-1809) by Chantrey, and of James Watt (1736-1819) by Flaxman. Boulton and Watt together established the famous Soho Manufactory at Smethwick in 1796 and it seems particularly appropriate that important busts of these nineteenth-century 'Renaissance men' should return to the scene of their most important joint venture, where they will be displayed at Soho House, Boulton's home, now owned by Birmingham City Council and due to open to the public in October 1995. This transaction was again completed via the offer *in lieu* arrangement. So was the acquisition by the National Trust for Scotland of a substantial part of the contents of Castle Fraser in Aberdeenshire. This was an excellent example of use of this arrangement to secure for the Nation chattels that are not necessarily of prime importance but nonetheless have a strong association with a particular house vested in the National Trust or some other heritage body.

The Ipswich Borough Council Museums acquired by private treaty an important collection of jewellery and coins dating from the seventh century. These items were excavated at Boss Hall in Ipswich from a burial site thought to date from the same era as the site excavated at Sutton Hoo and to have connections with the dynasty who ruled East Anglia at this time, members of which were buried at Sutton Hoo.

Among the more unusual items sold by private treaty were a set of medieval orphreys which passed to the Victoria & Albert Museum where they had been on loan for some years. These elaborate pieces, dating from the middle of the fourteenth century and forming a part of an ecclesiastical vestment, are worked in gold thread and brightly coloured silk. The front panel depicts Saint Andrew with three other male saints and incorporates the arms of John Grandison (1292-1369), Bishop of Exeter. The back orphrey portrays the Virgin Mary, Christ holding the Banner of the Resurrection, and three female saints. Grandison, a magnificent but turbulent priest, carried out major embellishments of Exeter Cathedral, this notwithstanding his aversion to Devonians, whom he denounced as being 'enemies of God and the Church'. Few other artistic products of this country have achieved wider fame than English embroidery of the Middle Ages. Particularly in the thirteenth and fourteenth centuries it was sought after by the great and good of Europe, and the Vatican Inventory of 1295 includes more pieces of Opus Anglicanum than any other kind of embroidery. Sadly, little of this rich and intricate work survives, much in England being destroyed during the Reformation, and much of that which was exported simply being worn out from years of use.

It is hoped that what is reported above may encourage both owners who have to dispose of objects and the curators of our museums to make use of the procedures relating to negotiated sales, which can provide benefits for each side and for the public at large.

# THE RUDOLF NUREYEV SALE

## by David Llewellyn

'Spirit of Nureyev turns auction into gala show' was *The Times* headline to its report of a remarkable sale. How fitting it was that the evening sale which started the proceedings was devoted almost exclusively to the Ballet, when costumes, blouses, boots and slippers were offered to a public that used to love and revere him when he danced. For once, this performance, witnessed by a truly international assembly of press and television, was a non-ticket event. The amphitheatre would mix with the stalls. For those that wanted the prized seats in the main saleroom, Christie's operated a policy of first come, first served. The later arrivals would be linked by television and a second auctioneer in the adjoining gallery. So it was that a line began to form at Christie's front door at 3.00 p.m. for the 7.00 p.m. 'show' which stretched from Park Avenue, down East 59th Street and into Madison Avenue. 'We used to form lines like this when he performed so why not now?' one fan was heard to explain. When Christopher Burge, the principal auctioneer and Nureyev's conductor for that evening, entered the rostrum he viewed an audience of which only a few could be recognised. In every sense this would be a different sale. Just over one hundred lots of this first session took nearly three hours to sell so fierce was the competition, as one determined fan was persuaded to go one step further than another. A friendly rivalry developed between bidders in the main room and others in the gallery. Bidders were applauded when successful. Some even congratulated themselves as others laughed and cheered. It was a joyous occasion, 'like a first night' as Burge remarked, and one which Nureyev would have undoubtedly enjoyed.

The costumes offered in the evening sale related to many of the principal roles and major productions of Nureyev's career ranging from the Princes of his classical repertoire (*Swan Lake, The Sleeping Beauty*) to the Ballets Russes de Diaghilev (*Le Spectre de la Rose* and *L'Après-midi d'un Faune*) and the modern idiom (*Pierrot Lunaire*). The glamour of the bejewelled costumes attracted some extraordinary prices but it came as no surprise when the highest price of all was reserved for perhaps the plainest in appearance. An ordinary and simple 'tunic of fawn stockinette piped in brown wool with false shirt' realised $51,750 (see p.220). It was in this

costume for Prince Albrecht in Act I of *Giselle* that Nureyev first performed with Margot Fonteyn on 21 February 1962, the start of one of the most remarkable partnerships in the history of dance.

Nureyev owned six properties throughout the world – a house near Nice, an island off Positano near Naples, a farm in Virginia and apartments in Paris, Monte Carlo and in the Dakota in New York: the contents of the last mentioned provided much that was offered in the second sale. The tall-ceilinged and large rooms of the Dakota provided ample space for Nureyev to house and display the grandest of his pictures and pieces of furniture to their greatest theatrical effect. The salon walls exemplified the diversity of Nureyev's taste. Late eighteenth- and early nineteenth-century male academies by Félix Boisselier and Joseph Galvan contrasted with the superbly theatrical, if not balletic, picture by Johann Heinrich Fuseli, *Satan starting from the Touch of Ithuriel's Lance* ($761,500). In its position over the fireplace Sir Joshua Reynolds' *Portrait of George Townshend, Lord de Ferrars* ($772,500, p. 6) dominated the room with its classical restraint, the *déhanchement* pose modelled on the antique and echoing that of the first century A.D. Roman marble torso of the *Diadumenos* after Polykleitos ($310,500, p. 167) that Nureyev placed in powerful isolation on a plinth in the centre of the room.

Through the rooms of the Dakota apartment contrasts abounded. The solid dark colours of Jacobean oak mixed with the lighter colour of Karelian birch and the pale upholstery on the pair of modern sofas from the collection of Maria Callas. From under the bed and out of the chests came textiles from every region of the world; kilims from Anatolia and Thrace, shawls from Kashmir, textiles from Japan and eighteenth-century dresses and waistcoats from the continent of Europe. Alexander Bland described Nureyev as being 'musical to his finger tips', a fact amply demonstrated by the Jacob Kirckman double manual harpsichord of 1760 that dominated the bedroom at the Dakota and undoubtedly appealed to Nureyev as a superb example of the marriage of the decorative and musical arts.

The richness and variety of Nureyev's collection allied to his own extraordinary and dynamic personality proved to be an irresistible attraction. The thousands that attended the view, that bought all available copies of the lavishly illustrated catalogue and that purchased in the sale relished in the opportunity to share in the collection put together with so much enthusiasm by one of the leading figures of the arts in the twentieth century. In many ways the sale was more than a gala. It was a celebration.

### JACOB KIRCKMAN
A double manual Harpsichord, London, 1760
30¾ in. (90.5 cm.) high; 37 in. (94 cm.) wide;
12¼ in. (31 cm.) deep; 92 in. (234 cm.) long
Sold by the Rudolf Nureyev Dance Foundation
New York, 13 January 1995, $94,775 (£64,447)

SIR JOSHUA REYNOLDS, P.R.A. (1723-1792)
Portrait of George Townshend, Lord de Ferrars (1755-1811)
oil on canvas, 94 x 56½ in. (238.7 x 143.5 cm.)
Sold by the Rudolf Nureyev Dance Foundation
New York, 13 January 1995, $772,500 (£525,300)

# PICTURES FROM HOUGHTON

## by Charles Beddington and Jo Hedley

A high point in the sale of works of art from Houghton Hall was unquestionably Jean-François de Troy's *La Lecture de Molière*. This delightful evocation of a Parisian interior at the time of the *Salons* has become one of the most popular and well known images of eighteenth-century French art.

All de Troy's early biographers emphasise the artist's personal social success among the wealthy sophisticated salon society of Paris in the 1720s and 1730s. He derived both inspiration and clientèle for his *tableaux de modes* among a select social group of which he himself was a privileged member, and it is probable that the present picture was commissioned by, or painted in the hope of attracting, a buyer from among this wealthy Parisian elite. The picture dates from the period between 1723 and 1737-8 when, as Mariette noted in 1762, de Troy 'a beaucoup plus à Paris pour ses petits tableaux de modes, qui sont en effet plus soignés que ses grands tableaux d'histoire'. The meticulous

JEAN-FRANÇOIS DE TROY (French, 1679-1752)
La Lecture de Molière
signed and dated '(D?)TROY./17(30?)'
oil on canvas
29⅛ x 36⅝ in. (74 x 93 cm.)
Sold from the collections of the Cholmondeley Family and the late Sir Philip Sassoon, Bt., from Houghton Hall, Norfolk
London, 8 December 1994, £3,961,500 ($6,195,786)
Record auction price for a work by the artist

rendition of the objects depicted within the picture itself help to date it yet more precisely. For instance, the *Régence* sconces above the mantlepiece belong to a period after 1723, the silver teapot is of a type in general use from 1717-18 onwards, and the pattern on the arabesque screen derives from an engraving by Boucher after Watteau's *Dénicheur de Moineaux* published in December 1727.

The picture was in the collection of Frederick the Great by 1733, when it was mentioned by M. Oesterreich in his *Description de tout l'intérieur de deux Palais de Sans Souci*. It was, together with its pendant *La Déclaration de l'Amour* (Potsdam, Sans Souci, signed and dated 1731), in the *seconde chambre* of the Royal Palace at Potsdam, which formed 'la chambre suivante' after the *chambre de concert*. Both pictures continued to hang together at Sans Souci until 1806 when, after the defeat of the Prussians by Napoleon, the present picture was seized on behalf of Baron Vivant Denon, the first Director of the Louvre.

How the picture passed into the collection of William, 2nd Earl of Lonsdale in the nineteenth century is still unclear, but its subsequent history is fully documented. In 1919 it passed from the Lonsdale collection into that of Sir Philip Sassoon, where it hung appropriately in the library of his London home at 25 Park Lane. On the latter's death, the work passed to Sir Philip's sister Sybil, wife of the 5th Marquess of Cholmondeley. It is one of the most scintillating examples of the originality and sophistication of de Troy's artistic vision, providing a brilliant visual counterpoint to the witty, epigrammatic salon literature of the day. Understandably, it has become an icon of French eighteenth-century art history;

SIR PETER PAUL RUBENS (Flemish, 1577-1640)
The Marriage by Proxy of Princess Maria de' Medici and King Henri IV of France in the Duomo, Florence, 5 October 1600 (*recto*); A Lion Hunt (*verso*) (*verso* illustrated)
oil on panel
19¾ x 17⅜ in. (50 x 44 cm.)
Sold from the collections of the Cholmondeley Family and the late Sir Philip Sassoon, Bt., from Houghton Hall, Norfolk
London, 8 December 1994, £1,761,500 ($2,754,986)
Record auction price for a work by the artist

reproduced in all the major histories of French art of the period, its power to please and fascinate is as strong as ever.

The Houghton sale also included a double-sided sketch by Rubens. He first used the panel for a sketch for *The Lion Hunt*, commissioned by John Digby, 1st Earl of Bristol for James, Marquess of Hamilton in 1621. The finished canvas is now in the Alte Pinakoteck, Munich.

Although the sketch for *The Lion Hunt* is unfinished, Professor Julius Held believes it to be 'the last comprehensive sketch' for the

picture. Held notes that the support was originally larger, and used in a horizontal format for a sketch of a hunt of which only the right part remains, largely indecipherable. Rubens then turned the support, which extended further to the left, upright and elaborated his ideas for *The Lion Hunt*. Subsequently, the artist decided to use the other side of the support and had it reduced. Finally turning the panel over, he sketched in vertical format the first *modello* for *The Marriage by Proxy of Princess Maria de' Medici*. This is a preparatory sketch for the eighth of the cycle of twenty-four canvases depicting the life of Maria de' Medici now in the Louvre. This cycle, commissioned by the then Queen Mother of France in 1622 to decorate the two galleries in the Palais du Luxembourg, was the most extensive and ambitious work yet undertaken by Rubens and was one of the most important commissions of his career.

The Rubens sketch was said to have been in the Major sale in London in 1751, when it sold to George, 3rd Earl of Cholmondeley (1703-1770). A more recent addition to the Houghton Collection was the superb pair of flower pieces by Jan van Os (£463,500). The first recorded owner, Lord Ward, later 1st Earl of Dudley, formed one of the finest collections in England

GIOVANNI BATTISTA CIPRIANI, R.A. (Italian, 1727-1785)
The Rape of Oreithyia
oil on canvas
83 x 68⅛ in. (210.8 x 173 cm.)
Sold from the collections of the Cholmondeley Family and the late Sir Philip Sassoon, Bt., from Houghton Hall, Norfolk
London, 8 December 1994, £199,500 ($312,018)
Record auction price for a work by the artist

of the mid-nineteenth century, including works by Fra Angelico, Raphael, Rembrandt, Frans van Mieris and Hobbema; these were sold at Christie's on 25 June 1892.

A further world record price was achieved for Cipriani's masterpiece *The Rape of Oreithyia*. Born in France, Cipriani was brought to London from Rome by Sir William Chambers and Joseph Wilton in 1756, and became one of the first painters to work in the Neo-classical style in England. *The Rape of Oreithyia*, which was exhibited at the Royal Academy in 1776, was acquired by George Walpole, 3rd Earl of Orford (1730-1791).

GIULIO PIPPI, called GIULIO ROMANO
(Italian, 1492/9-1546)
The Spinola Holy Family
oil on panel
29⅞ x 25 in. (76 x 63.5 cm.)
Sold from Wrotham Park
London, 9 December 1994, £1,541,500 ($2,404,740)

The Spinola *Holy Family*, although admired in the nineteenth century, evaded attention until it was published in 1982. It first appeared at Christie's when it was sold in 1826 for the Hon. Sir William Waldegrave, 1st Baron Radstock, to George Byng,

M.P. for 890 guineas, and it hung at Wrotham Park until it was sent for sale.

Giulio's fame now rests on his inventive facility, represented most obviously by the frescoes of the Palazzo del Tè, but it is on his adaptation of the art of the late Raphael that his significance in the mainstream of European painting depends and the Spinola picture is one of the key statements of this aspect of his oeuvre. Smaller, and thus more intimate in scale, than most of the compositions to which it is most directly related, the Spinola *Holy Family* must be marginally earlier in date than the *Stoning of Saint Stephen* of 1523 in the church of that Saint, Giulio's only documented Genoese commission, in which such details as the matted grasses are precisely paralleled.

FERNANDO YÁÑEZ DE LA ALMEDINA
(Spanish, active 1506-circa 1561)
The Nativity with a kneeling Donor
oil on panel
41 x 39 in. (104 x 99 cm.)
Monaco, 30 June 1995, Fr.2,700,500 (£348,902)

Fernando Yáñez de la Almedina, along with his compatriot Fernando Llanos, was to exercise a profound influence on the course of Valencian painting in the sixteenth century. Most scholars agree that it is to the former, the author of the *Nativity with a kneeling Donor*, that contemporary sources refer as assisting Leonardo da Vinci in his ill-fated project to adorn the Council Chamber of the Palazzo Vecchio in Florence. Indeed the references in this *Nativity* to Leonardo's work are striking, as witnessed in the outstretched left hand of the Virgin which recalls that in Leonardo's *Madonna of the Rocks*, or the similarity between the facial type of the Saint Joseph in the *Nativity* and Leonardo's pen drawings of grotesque heads at Windsor.

Despite the debt to his Italian master, Yáñez also imbued his composition with a quite individual vitality and freshness. In an exceptional state of preservation, this recently rediscovered panel, by an artist whose work is rarely seen on the market, doubled its top estimate.

AMBROSIUS BOSSCHAERT I (Flemish, 1573-1621)
Tulips, Narcissi, Roses, an Iris, Columbine, Fritillaries, Lilies,
a 'Goudlakense' Crocus, Forget-me-nots, an Anemone, a Marigold
and Sweet Briar in a glass Vase, with a Carnation, a Caterpillar,
a Fly and a Painted Lady on a Ledge
signed with monogram 'AB'
oil on copper
12⅛ x 9⅜ in. (30.7 x 23.8 cm.)
New York, 11 January 1995, $1,432,500 (£873,476)

*Right:*
PIETER BRUEGHEL II (Flemish, c. 1564-1637/8)
A Proverb: two jesters mocking each other in a landscape
oil on panel
7⅜ in. (18.9 cm.) diameter
Sold from the collection of the Heirs of A.J.Blijdenstein
Amsterdam, 8 May 1995, Fl.264,500 (£106,225)

ROELANT SAVERY (Flemish, 1576-1639)
Orpheus charming the Animals
signed 'R.Savery'
oil on panel
11⅞ x 16¼ in. (30 x 41.2 cm.)
Amsterdam, 17 November 1994, Fl.299,000 (£109,124)

GIROLAMO FRANCESCO MARIA MAZZOLA,
called PARMIGIANINO (Italian, 1503-1540)
The Madonna and Child
oil on panel
13⅜ x 17⅝ in. (34 x 44.8 cm.)
Sold by the Trustees of the Kedleston Estate Trusts
London, 7 July 1995, £881,500 ($1,405,111)
Record auction price for a work by the artist

This picture, which dates from the artist's period at Bologna, after the Sack of Rome in 1527, was acquired from the collection of Marchese Arnaldi at Florence in 1758 for Sir Nathaniel Curzon, 5th Bt., later 1st Baron Scarsdale.

CARLO DOLCI (Italian, 1616-1686)
Saint John the Evangelist
oil on canvas
40⅛ x 32½ in. (102.2 x 82.5 cm.)
New York, 11 January 1995, $398,500 (£242,988)

Carlo Dolci, a perennial favourite among British collectors, probably painted this *Saint John the Evangelist* for his confessor, Domenico Carpanti. It was later in the collections of the Riccardi at Palazzo Medici-Riccardi, Florence, Lucien Buonaparte, Sir Simon Clarke, and Lord Northwick, at whose sale in 1859 it fetched the highest price of 2,010 guineas.

JOHANN LISS (German, c.1597-c.1630)
A repentant Sinner turning away from Temptation and offered
a Palm of Salvation by an Angel
oil on canvas
38⅞ x 49½ in. (98.8 x 125.8 cm.)
London, 9 December 1994, £991,500 ($1,550,706)

Works by Johann Liss, a German artist who worked in the Netherlands, France and Italy during a brief life cut short at the age of thirty by the plague raging in Venice, are rare. Liss was, more than any of his contemporaries, a truly European painter. Along with Elsheimer, he was one of the few seventeenth-century German artists capable of stimulating the development of European art.

*The repentant Sinner*, or *Temptation of the Magdalen*, was probably painted in Rome after the artist left the Netherlands, but before he settled in Venice. It presumably reached England by the mid-eighteenth century and was framed as an overmantle of the former Billiard Room at Edgcote in Northamptonshire until 1925. Hitherto known only from an old photograph, it was previously believed to be a copy after a version in Dresden.

JOHANN LISS (German, c. 1597-c. 1630)
Christ in the Garden
signed and dated 'Ioañes.liss:F./A:D:i(6)2.:' and signed on the
reverse 'Johann Liss'
oil on copper
11⅛ x 8¼ in. (28.2 x 21 cm.)
London, 7 July 1995, £518,500 ($826,489)

The appearance of the second picture by Liss during the same
auction season provided an opportunity to see a different aspect of
the artist's output. *Christ in the Garden*, unique in that it is the only
signed and dated painting by the artist, was painted in the last years
of Liss's life. The jewel-like quality of this picture with its contrast
of dense colours, sparkling light and the small-scale format and use
of a copper support reflects Liss's continuing kinship with his fellow
countryman, Adam Elsheimer.

# THE CAREL GOLDSCHMIDT COLLECTION

## by Peter C. Sutton

'The United Provinces [of the Netherlands] are the envy of some, the fear of others, and the wonder of all their neighbors.'
Sir William Temple (English Ambassador to the Netherlands, *Observations upon the United Provinces*, 1673.)

Long celebrated for its truth to life, technical brilliance, and unembellished subject matter, seventeenth-century Dutch painting was an exceptional art form in absolutist Europe – one created not for monarchs or the mighty but primarily for a community of burghers at once enterprising and industrious, practical and tolerant. During their 'Golden Age' the Dutch not only successfully held their larger neighbours at bay, but also thrived as the hub of a far flung trading empire, indeed became the richest society per capita in all of Christendom. Sheer prosperity and openness would defy the despots. Yet for all their wealth, the Dutch seemed to outsiders (especially visiting Frenchmen) remarkably abstemious, frugal and chaste. In the newly independent Protestant Republic, the home rather than the Church was the primary forum of moral instruction and became a sort of secular temple. Domesticity was prized above all other virtues and the family advanced as the primary social unit, the sacred essence of civilization. It is perhaps not surprising, therefore, that the naturalistic scenes of everyday life, the simple landscapes and fastidiously observed still lifes of Dutch painting have long appealed to successful men of affairs.

Born in Amsterdam, Carel Goldschmidt (1904-1989) prospered in tobacco and other investments with his lifelong partner, Theodore Cremer, and both men took special pleasure in collecting Dutch art. On 11 January 1995, Christie's sold the Goldschmidt collection and its exceptional group of cabinet-sized paintings and drawings. The highlight of the sale was a brilliant little painting of a peasant family in a cottage interior by the foremost Dutch painter of low life themes, Adriaen Jansz. van Ostade (1610-1685). Seated at a table with the left-overs of a meal, the comfortably stout and smiling couple dandle their toddler while two other children play by the gentle light of a mullioned window. In this eminently unpretentious even ramshackle interior, Ostade has lavished all his remarkable powers of observation on the most commonplace of still life details – a spinner's cast off equipment, a wicker crib and crushed basket, coarse rags, a wooden beer keg, broken ceramics and kitchen utensils. Rarely has such a quotidian scene been so lovingly recorded.

Ostade executed several similar paintings, drawings and prints of contented peasant families in modest settings; the closest in conception of these to the present work is the painting dated 1668 in the collection of H.M. Queen Elizabeth II at Buckingham Palace. A seventeenth-century print after one of Ostade's lost paintings of this theme was inscribed 'Yet we love our little child from the heart and that is no trifle/Thus we regard our miserable hovel as a splendid mansion', suggesting that the joys of family life compensated for the deprivations of poverty.

Evidently Ostade regarded the domestic virtues, then championed for the upper and middle classes by Jacob Cats (1577-1650) and other Dutch moralists, as valid for the peasantry as well. Ostade himself had known modest beginnings as the third of eight children born to a weaver in Haarlem.

We are told by the seventeenth-century chronicler of artists' lives, Arnold Houbraken, that he was a pupil of Frans Hals together with the famous Flemish peasant painter, Adriaen Brouwer (1606-1638). Brouwer had a demonstrable influence on Ostade's earlier style. However, whereas Brouwer personally suffered financial difficulties and even spent time in prison, by the time Ostade painted the present picture, he had married well and prospered. In the same year, 1661, he was also elected head of the local painters' guild for a second time. Thus the known facts of his life, like those of his famous sixteenth-century predecessor among peasant painters, Pieter Bruegel, serve to refute the familiar biographical fallacy that assumes a painter's art must illustrate his life.

Despite the painting's low life theme, it was later owned by several of the most prominent eighteenth-century collectors of Northern paintings among the Dutch and French aristocracy (Count van Wassenaar-van Obdam, who owned no less than eleven Ostades, the duc de Choiseul, and the prince de Conti) and was subsequently in the famous collection of Robert Staynor Holford (1808-1892), the most expensive collection sold at auction (1928) prior to the Second World War.

Among the other outstanding Dutch paintings in the Goldschmidt collection were landscapes by Jan van Goyen and Jacob van Ruisdael. The latter's dramatic wooded mountainous landscape dated 1653 was executed shortly after Ruisdael's *wanderjahr* in Westphalia and handsomely evokes the local scenery and architecture. The drawings also included a large group of van Goyen's black chalk sketches, an excellent single figure study by Ostade, as well as a colourful scene of skittle players at an inn by Ostade's pupil, Cornelis Dusart (1660-1704). However, the highlight of the drawings was a brush and brown wash drawing of *A seated young Boy in a Hat*, his chin cupped in his hand (see p.28), by Rembrandt's pupil, Gerbrand van den Eeckhout (1621-1674). Rembrandt and Eeckhout were close and the latter followed his master's style for longer than most of his fellow pupils. Of the approximately sixteen such sheets surviving, this contemplative image is one of Eeckhout's own personal manner. The boy's momentary, self-absorbed expression epitomizes Dutch naturalism at its most casual and plausible.

ADRIAEN JANSZ. VAN OSTADE (Dutch, 1610-1685)
A Peasant Family in the Interior of a Cottage
signed and dated 'Av Ostade 1661'
oil on panel
13½ x 12 in. (34.9 x 31.1 cm.)
Sold from the Carel Goldschmidt Collection
New York, 11 January 1995, $1,982,500 (£1,270,833)
Record auction price for a work by the artist

PAULUS POTTER (Dutch, 1625-1654)
Cattle in a Field, with Travellers in a Wagon on a Track Beyond
and a Church Tower in the Distance, a rain storm approaching
signed and dated 'Paulus Potter.F:1652'
oil on panel
14¾ x 22 in. (37.5 x 56 cm.)
London, 7 July 1995, £661,500 ($1,054,431)
Record auction price for a work by the artist

'Plus qu'aucun peintre en cette école honnête il parla de náïveté, de
patience, de circonspection, d'amour persévérant pour le vrai.'
(More than any other painter of this honest school, he spoke of
naiveté, patience, circumspection and the persevering love of
truth; Eugène Fromentin, *Les Maîtres d'Autrefois*, 1876.)

For the nineteenth century, Paulus Potter epitomized the
Dutchman's devotion to fact and careful observation. Indeed the
artist and author, Fromentin, sought to portray Potter as an artistic
ingénu who recorded the simple facts of his animal subjects and
landscapes virtually automatically, betraying not the least concern
with style or pictorial convention. The minute finish and
extraordinary fidelity to nature in Potter's *Cattle in a Field* of 1652
would seem to vindicate Fromentin's claim that 'the slightest
artifice would have been an embarrassment' ('le moindre artifice
était un embarras') to Potter. However, such a pictorial
achievement is scarcely the result of empirical observation alone.
The few known facts of Potter's short life do not bear out his latter-
day image as a naive autodidact. Though a youthful prodigy, he
was a well educated and sophisticated man who not only enjoyed
elevated social connections but also the patronage of the court in
The Hague as well as leading families in Amsterdam. Yet there
remains a poetic truth in the nineteenth century's celebration of

him as the paradigm of realism when one considers this remarkably
unsentimental image of cattle lowing beside a moss-covered tree
before the darkening skies of a spring storm. When exhibited in
1995 in the monographic exhibition devoted to Potter, this
brilliantly fastidious little cabinet-sized painting was singled out as
'one of the highpoints of Potter's oeuvre'.

*Right:*
GASPAR VAN WITTEL, called GASPARE VANVITELLI
(Dutch, 1653-1736)
Castel Sant' Angelo and Ponte Sant' Angelo, Rome, looking east
from the Gardens of the Hospital of Santo Spirito in Sassia with
Santa Trinità dei Monti and the Villa Medici beyond
oil on canvas
33½ x 45 in. (85 x 114.3 cm.)
New York, 18 May 1995, $827,500 (£471,675)
Record auction price for a work by the artist

JACOB BOGDANI (Hungarian, c.1660-1724)
Muscovy Ducks, a Ruff, a Curlew and Scarlet Ibis in a wooded
Landscape
signed 'J.Bogdani'
36¼ x 52¼ in. (93.4 x 133.2 cm.)
Sold from the collection of Jeremy Cotton, Esq., Tythrop Park
London, 27 April 1995, £232,500 ($375,022)
One of a group of works by Bogdani sold for a total of
£1,160,000 ($1,867,600)

GIOVANNI ANTONIO CANAL, II CANALETTO
(Italian, 1697-1768)
The Island of San Giorgio Maggiore and the Bacino di San
Marco, Venice, from the Riva degli Schiavoni
oil on canvas
23⅝ x 37¼ in. (60 x 94.5 cm.)
New York, 11 January 1995, $2,092,500 (£1,275,915)

No other version of Canaletto's view of the *Island of San Giorgio
Maggiore and the Bacino di San Marco, Venice* is known, which is
unusual as the artist was inclined to repeat popular compositions.
Canaletto's genius at organising a view into a unified whole, while
at the same time incorporating a mass of detail, is nowhere more
apparent than in this picture. The artist's almost reverential
treatment of the architecture of Venice is seen in the clean and pure
lines of Andrea Palladio's façade of San Giorgio Maggiore, and set
off by the bustling activity of the merchants, noblemen, and
gondoliers on the Riva degli Schiavoni in the foreground.

*Right:*
BERNARDO BELLOTTO (Italian, 1721-1780)
Santa Maria della Salute and the Entrance to the Grand Canal,
Venice, looking East from the Campo Santa Maria Zobenigo,
with the Palazzo Pisani-Gritti, barges and numerous gondolas,
the Dogana and the Riva degli Schiavoni beyond
oil on canvas
24½ x 38 in. (72 x 96.5 cm.)
New York, 11 January 1995, $1,322,500 (£806,402)

MICHELE MARIESCHI (Italian, 1710-1744)
The Campo San Gallo, Venice
oil on canvas
38¾ x 54⅛ in. (98.5 x 137.5 cm.)
London, 9 December 1994, £463,500 ($724,914)

# OLD MASTER DRAWINGS

**LEONARDO DA VINCI** (Italian, 1452-1519)
Caricature of the Head of an old Man, in profile to the right
pen and brown ink
4¼ x 3⅛ in. (11 x 8 cm.)
London, 4 July 1995, £221,500 ($352,185)

The most important of Leonardo's grotesques to appear on the
market since the Chatsworth sale in 1984, this drawing was
previously sold at Christie's in 1963 for 14,000 guineas. It may
be dated circa 1507 and its extraordinary delicacy of execution
recalls Leonardo's silverpoint technique, here translated into pen
and ink. The subject is more than simply a portrait of a
disfigured old man, but reflects Leonardo's deeper interest in
physiognomy – the study of human character through the
features. The drawing previously belonged to three
distinguished English collectors: the Earl of Arundel, the
painter Jonathan Richardson and John Bouverie.

**ALONSO BERRUGUETE** (Spanish, 1486-1561)
Study of a draped Man
pen and black ink
10½ x 5⅞ in. (26.5 x 15 cm.)
Monaco, 30 June 1995, Fr.370,900 (£48,044)
Now in the Musée du Louvre, Paris

This study of a seated man is a significant addition to the small corpus of
drawings by Berruguete, the most important Spanish sculptor of the
sixteenth century, who studied in Italy with Michelangelo. It probably
relates to one of the reliefs of the choir of the Cathedral of Toledo
commissioned by the canons of the Cathedral in 1543.

PIETRO BERRETTINI, called
PIETRO DA CORTONA
(Italian, 1596-1669)
Cybele before the Council of the Gods
black chalk, pen and brown ink, brown
wash, heightened with white
7¾ x 5¾ in. (19.5 x 14.5 cm.)
Sold from the Stichting Collectie
P. en N. de Boer
London, 4 July 1995, £91,700 ($145,803)

GIAMPIETRO ZANOTTI
(Italian, 1674-1765)
The Accademia Clementina,
Bologna, with a Nude being
positioned by the Drawing Master
black chalk, pen and brown ink,
brown wash
3⅝ x 5½ in. (9.4 x 13.8 cm.)
Sold from the Stichting Collectie
P. en N. de Boer
London, 4 July 1995, £24,150 ($38,399)

The Foundation de Boer was established
in Amsterdam in 1960 by Pieter de Boer
(1896-1974) who had begun to form his
collection in the 1940s. The sale at
Christie's of the Italian and other
drawings secured funds for the
conservation of the core of the
collection, which concentrates on Dutch
and Flemish art.

Two of the highlights from the
collection were works by Pietro da
Cortona and Giampietro Zanotti. The
former was engraved by Greuter for
one of the earliest books on gardening,
*De Florum Cultura*, 1633, written by
Giovanni Battista Ferrari, a Sienese Jesuit
from the circle of Cardinal Francesco
Barberini, nephew of Urban VIII.
Through the Cardinal's secretary,
Cassiano dal Pozzo, other artists like Sacchi
and Reni also became involved in the
project. The second drawing is by the little-
known Bolognese master Giampietro
Zanotti, who was one of the founders
and the first secretary of the Accademia
Clementina. The drawing was engraved
by the artist himself as the frontispiece of
the second volume of his *Storia dell'
Accademia Clementina di Bologna*, 1739.
The book traces the history of Bolognese
painting from Malvasia's *Felsina Pittrice*,
published in 1686, to the foundation of
the Accademia in 1706.

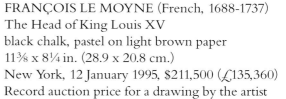

FRANÇOIS LE MOYNE (French, 1688-1737)
The Head of King Louis XV
black chalk, pastel on light brown paper
11⅜ x 8¼ in. (28.9 x 20.8 cm.)
New York, 12 January 1995, $211,500 (£135,360)
Record auction price for a drawing by the artist

A study for the head of the King for *Louis XV donnant la paix à l'Europe* commissioned for Versailles in 1729 by the *Directeur Général des Bâtiments du Roi*, the duc d'Antin. The commission of this allegorical portrait proved important for Le Moyne as it was the first of a series that led four years later to his appointment as first painter to the King, a prestigious post also coveted by his rival Jean-François de Troy. The King at that time was nineteen years old, and Cardinal de Fleury, his prime minister, was at the peak of his power: the alliance he concluded with the government of Walpole allowed him to re-establish peace between the Emperor Charles VI and the King of Spain. This pastel, one of a handful known by Le Moyne, was probably executed from life, in one sitting, and later used in the picture.

FRANÇOIS BOUCHER (French, 1703-1770)
Head of a Woman seen from behind
red, black and white chalk on light brown paper
11⅜ x 9¼ in. (28.8 x 23.6 cm.)
Sold by the Trustees of the late Viscountess Ward of Witley
London, 4 July 1995, £177,500 ($282,225)

Boucher used this striking drawing of a nymph seen from behind in two works, both executed circa 1737. The nymph appears first testing the sharpness of an arrow, in the foreground of an overdoor of the *Education of Cupid* that was part of a series of three, painted for the duchesse de Meillaraye for the hôtel de Mazarin in Paris. The same figure reappears in the middle ground of a tapestry on the *Story of Psyche* commissioned by the French Crown in 1737. The figure being absent in all the compositional studies for the tapestries, it must have been added to the design at the last moment: the artist evidently drew on his existing stock of figure studies.

JEAN-ETIENNE LIOTARD (Swiss, 1702-1789)
A Woman in Turkish Costume in a *Hamam* instructing her Servant
pastel
27⅝ x 22¼ in. (70.3 x 56.3 cm.)
London, 4 July 1995, £903,500 ($1,436,565)
Record auction price for a pastel by the artist

This pastel dates from after Liotard's return from Constantinople in 1742. He had arrived in the city after a trip around the Mediterranean with Lord Duncannon and the Earl of Sandwich.

On his arrival Liotard soon became acquainted with various English merchants and was able to draw numerous notables such as the Grand Vizier and Lady Tyrrell, the wife of the British Consul, whose portrait was sold at Christie's in 1991 for a then record price. Upon his return to Europe Liotard continued to dress *à la Turque* and called himself 'le peintre turc'. This unusual depiction of a woman and her servant in front of a washbasin in a *hamam* characterises, in the precise rendering of the silk dresses and jewellery, Liotard's interest in exotic costumes. At the same sale *La belle Liseuse*, another pastel by Liotard, was sold for £331,500 ($527,085).

GERBRAND VAN DEN EECKHOUT
(Dutch, 1621-1674)
A seated young Boy in a Hat, his chin cupped in
his hand
brush and brown wash, brown ink framing lines
5½ x 4½ in. (14 x 11.5 cm.)
Sold from the Carel Goldschmidt Collection
New York, 12 January 1995,
$365,500 (£233,920)
Record auction price for a drawing by the artist

The Carel Goldschmidt Collection is discussed
by Peter Sutton on pp. 18-19.

CONSTANTIJN HUYGENS
(Dutch, 1628-1697)
View of The Hague from the North with
Grote Kerk to the right, and to its left the
Tower of the Townhall, the Kloosterkerk, part
of the Oude Hof at the Noordeinde, and the
nearby Engelse and Hoogduitse Kerk
black lead, pen and brown ink, brown wash
8⅝ x 15¼ in. (22 x 38.8 cm.)
Amsterdam, 14 November 1994,
Fl.218,500 (£79,310)

ALBRECHT DÜRER (German, 1471-1528)
A Coat of Arms with a Skull (Bartsch 101)
engraving, a rich Meder Ia impression
P. 8¾ x 6¼ in. (22.4 x 16.1 cm.)
London, 29 November 1994, £62,000 ($96,782)

In conception and execution this is one of Dürer's finest prints. A young woman, gently smiling and still wearing her bridal crown, is tenderly embraced by Death, here portrayed as the wild man of Swiss and German myth. The lady does not recognise his true identity and does not reject him. Nevertheless, the skull on the shield confronts the viewer as a relentless memento mori.

In this enigmatic and subtle allegory of Love and Death, Dürer lovingly describes the different textures of feathers, metal and drapery. The plume of the helmet in particular is a bravura display of technique.

# BRITISH PICTURES

SIR JOSHUA REYNOLDS, P.R.A. (1723-1792)
Portrait of Oliver Goldsmith (1728-1774)
oil on canvas
30 x 25¼ in. (76.2 x 64.1 cm.)
Sold by the Trustees of the Bedford Estates
London, 11 November 1994, £89,500 ($143,200)
Now in the National Gallery of Ireland, Dublin

Reynolds' first portrait of Goldsmith was commissioned by the Duke of Dorset and exhibited at the Royal Academy in 1770 with a companion portrait of Dr. Samuel Johnson. Believed to have been executed in 1772, this version was one of a series commissioned by Henry Thrale, a wealthy brewer and M.P. who regularly entertained members of Johnson's literary circle in his house at Streatham.

*Above:*
JOHN E. FERNELEY, SEN.
(1782-1860)
Tom Hodgson and Alexander
Bosville, with a Huntsman and
Hounds in the Great Pasture,
Thorpe
signed and dated
'J. Ferneley/Melton Mowbray/
1836'
oil on canvas
44½ x 63¼ in. (113 x 160.7 cm.)
Sold from the collection of
Sir Ian MacDonald of Sleat, Bt.
London, 8 June 1995,
£199,500 ($317,205)

JOHN FREDERICK
HERRING, SEN. (1795-1865)
Horses, a Goat, Doves and a
Pigeon outside a Barn
signed and dated
'J.F.Herring Sen. 1848'
oil on canvas
40 x 50 in. (101.6 x 127 cm.)
London, 11 November 1994,
£128,000 ($204,800)

# A MASTERPIECE BY STUBBS

## by John Stainton

In its presence and brooding power, George Stubbs' *Portrait of The Royal Tiger* is something of an icon of the 'golden age' of British animal painting. The largest of three depictions of the animal, James Barry commented that the subject 'must rouse and agitate the most inattentive' while Fuseli remarked of Stubbs: 'His tiger for Grandeur has never been equalled.'

Wild animals in general, and particularly those brought back from distant travels, held a great fascination for people in the eighteenth century. The beast depicted in the *Portrait of The Royal Tiger* was given to George Spencer, 4th Duke of Marlborough by Lord Clive, Governor of Bengal, in 1762-3. The tiger, which is thought to have been a female of the species, was installed in the menagerie at Blenheim Palace and a bill dated 1763, recording the delivery of 24 pounds of meat for the tiger every two or three days at a cost of three shillings a time, is still in the Blenheim archives.

Stubbs executed three portraits of the animal, each showing it in the same pose though on different scales. The first, exhibited at the Society of Artists in 1769, is believed to be that still in the Marlborough Collection at Blenheim (40 x 50 in.), and was the picture after which John Dixon executed his famous print of *A Tigress* (1772), described by *The Monthly Magazine* as 'The finest mezzotint that was ever engraved'. Another version (24 x 28 in.) is now in the collection of Mr. and Mrs. Paul Mellon and, as with the Blenheim picture, uses the same basic composition, but with small variations in the background, and differing vegetation in the foreground. The Portman work is, however, by far the largest of the three and, as a monumental animal picture, can be compared with the artist's near life-size portraits of stallions such as *Whistlejacket*, *Scrub* and *Hambletonian*.

We are enormously grateful to Mrs. Judy Egerton, who arranged the definitive exhibition on Stubbs held at the Tate Gallery in 1984-5, for contributing a superb entry for the *Portrait of The Royal Tiger* in our sale catalogue. In this she remarked of the animal: 'It is observed with the underlying knowledge of anatomy which Stubbs had acquired a decade or more earlier through his studious dissection of the anatomy of the horse; but this tiger is not painted with pure scientific detachment. Stubbs brought the full force of his imagination to bear on suggesting the latent power within the animal.' Mrs. Egerton continues: 'Though the tigress is depicted reclining and apparently replete ... Stubbs leaves us in little doubt that if menaced, the tiger would spring to attack with one lithe and supremely co-ordinated bound. This inherant sense of danger in one of nature's most formidable creations links Stubbs' *Tiger* with subjects in the natural world which contemporaries deemed to be 'sublime', since they aroused emotions of awe and fear. Twelve years before Stubbs' death, William Blake composed and illustrated what are certainly the best-known lines about a tiger in English literature, as Stubbs' image is the best-known in English art:

> 'Tyger Tyger, burning bright,
> In the forests of the night;
> What immortal hand or eye,
> Could frame thy fearful symmetry?'
> (*Songs of Experience*, 1794.)

'But Blake's image of the tiger (standing) owes no direct debt to Stubbs, and appears rather to derive from Thomas Bewick's woodcuts of wild cats. Stubbs' tiger is observed with all the truthfulness to nature which the artist himself consistently declared to be his guiding principle. The eyes themselves reflect, unforgettably, this truthfulness. Unwavering in the gaze they turn upon us, they appear as uncommunicative as rock crystal. The quasi-human emotions with which Landseer imbued his animals have no place here. Stubbs instead conveys his knowledge that the tiger will respond, swiftly enough, and purely (in both senses of the word) to the laws of nature.

'Above all, Stubbs brought his skills as a painter to bear on the body of the tiger, suggesting the muscles beneath the skin, and painting the stripes of the coat with a controlled virtuosity which, two centuries later, still suggests the delicate play of filtered sunlight over the vibrant black and yellow of the tiger's coat. The subtlety of the paint is seen to most telling effect in daylight.'

Stubbs' audience was certainly well aware of the latent power of wild animals. In 1757, Mrs. Delany reported that the Duke of Cumberland's tiger had escaped its den and 'tore a boy of eight or nine years of age to pieces'. A rather more light-hearted incident occured when, in 1764, the Duke staged an encounter in Windsor Great Park between a stag and a cheetah, which had been given to his nephew, King George III, by Sir George Pigot, and is the subject of Stubbs' *A Cheetah and a Stag with Two Indians*, now in the Manchester City Art Gallery. The Duke's objective was to observe how the animal would tackle its prey but, after three failed attacks, the cheetah fled into the woods where it later killed a fallow deer, thereby fulfilling the purpose of the demonstration if in a rather unforseen manner. Incidents such as these give some impression of the contemporary fascination with, and sense of awe for, such animals and, with his Tiger, one can understand how Stubbs sought to transcend the traditional limitations of animal painting, just as contemporary landscape painters responded to concepts of the sublime and artists such as Reynolds set out to raise portraiture to a higher plane.

To some degree, the *raison d'être* of the Portman picture remains a mystery. Although thought to have been executed in the early 1770s, the *Portrait of The Royal Tiger* remained in Stubbs' studio until his death on 10 July 1806. While we might imagine that the work's execution followed a favourable response shown to the Blenheim picture (which had been exhibited in 1769), the intriguing, albeit unanswerable, question is raised as to whether the monumental version had been painted speculatively or as a commission which fell through. In either case, the picture's importance was unquestioned, for on the second day of the artist's studio sale in May 1807, it fetched the enormous sum of 350 guineas – by far the highest price achieved on either day of the sale.

*Portrait of The Royal Tiger* was lent by the 2nd Viscount Portman to the Winter Exhibition at the Royal Academy in 1892, and was not subsequently on public view until it was placed on loan to the Tate Gallery in 1947-1961. It was during this period that the picture was included in two important exhibitions – *George Stubbs*, at the Walker Art Gallery, Liverpool, in 1951; and *The Romantic Movement*, at the Tate in 1959.

GEORGE STUBBS, A.R.A. (1724-1806)
*Portrait of The Royal Tiger*
signed 'Geo:Stubbs/pinxit'
oil on canvas
55 x 85 in. (139.7 x 215.9 cm.)
Sold by the Trustees of the Portman Family
London, 8 June 1995, £3,191,500 ($5,061,719)
Record auction price for a work by the artist

# BRITISH DRAWINGS AND WATERCOLOURS

THOMAS GAINSBOROUGH, R.A. (1727-1788)
A Mountain Landscape with Herdsman and Cattle passing a Cottage
black and white chalk and stump on buff paper
11 x 14½ in. (27.9 x 38.8 cm.)
Sold by the Trustees of the Holker Estates
London, 8 November 1994, £91,700 ($148,554)

This is one of a number of studies made by Gainsborough under
the influence of Gaspard Poussin in the mid-1780s.

*Top right:*
RICHARD PARKES BONINGTON (1802-1828)
Dunkirk from the Sea
signed 'R P Bonington' and indistinctly dated '182(?)'
pencil and watercolour heightened with scratching out
6¼ x 9½ in. (15.9 x 24.2 cm.)
London, 25 April 1995, £80,700 ($129,120)

This recently discovered work is one of a group of water-colours of
Dunkirk usually dated to circa 1824.

*Bottom right:*
SAMUEL PALMER, O.W.S. (1805-1881)
Illustration to Milton's *Lycidas*
signed indistinctly and inscribed on the reverse
'This is a 6 sheet London Board/I advise that it should never be
thinned/by removing paper from the back/Stoutness increases
permanence and lustre/S.Palmer'
watercolour heightened with bodycolour
15½ x 23 in. (39.4 x 58.4 cm.)
London, 11 July 1995, £89,500 ($142,215)

Palmer's interest in Milton had been influenced, from childhood,
by his nurse, Mary Ward. In 1855 and 1856 Palmer exhibited
three watercolours illustrating Milton's *Comus* at the Old Water
Colour Society. In 1864, stimulated by commissions from Ruskin's
solicitor Leonard Rowe Valpy, he began a series of illustrations to
*L'Allegro* and *Il Penseroso*. This watercolour, smaller in size,
seems to have been a by-product of the series and was included
in a posthumous publication of Palmer's illustrations to Milton's
*Shorter Poems* in 1889.

JAMES STEPHANOFF, O.W.S. (1788-1874)
The Ascent of the Arts: An Assemblage of Works of Art in Sculpture
and Painting from the earliest Period to the Time of Phydias
pencil and watercolour
29¼ x 24½ in. (74.3 x 62.2 cm.)
London, 8 November 1994, £73,000 ($118,260)
Record auction price for a work by the artist
Now in the British Museum

Between 1817 and 1845 Stephanoff exhibited a series of six large
watercolours at the Society of Painters in Water-Colours, all of

them displaying in a didactic manner works of art taken from the
collection of the British Museum. This example includes
specimens of Hindu and Javanese sculpture, bas-reliefs from
Copan and Babylon as well as Egyptian, Etruscan and early
Greek remains.

It has been suggested by Ian Jenkins that Stephanoff was
following contemporary ideas on the evolution of art, demonstrat-
ing the progress from Oriental works in the lowest register to the
perfection of classical Greece. In this he was reflecting a knowledge
of Hegel's *Philosophy of Fine Art*, 1836, though Hegel saw a
progression from symbolic through Classic to Romantic Art.

AGRA SCHOOL, circa 1815
The Taj Mahal from the Garden
pencil, pen and grey ink and watercolour heightened with white
21 x 26¾ in. (53.4 x 68 cm.)
Sold from the collection of Paul F. Walter
London, 25 May 1995, £25,300 ($39,974)
From an album of drawings sold for a total of £147,430 ($232,644)

After the British captured Delhi and Agra in 1803, the demand for
pictures of monuments in this area grew. Amateurs found it difficult to
record the intricacy of Mughal architecture and local Indian artists
were commissioned to provide more accurate drawings. The 'Visions of
India' sale was Christie's first auction of works related to the Raj.
Following its success, another sale is scheduled for next year.

*Right:*
SAMUEL DUKINFIELD SWARBRECK (active 1830-1850)
View of Prince Albert's Swiss Cottage
signed, inscribed and dated 1847, pencil and watercolour heightened
with white, 18 x 13¾ in. (45.7 x 34.9 cm.)
London, 17 November 1994, £29,900 ($47,002)
Record auction price for a work by the artist

Christie's first sale devoted to views of interiors was an outstanding
success. The sale chronicled the changing taste and style in interior
decoration across Europe and America from the seventeenth century to
the present day. Interiors will now become a regular auction category
at Christie's, forming part of the sale programme in London.

JOSEPH WOLF (1820-1899)
Snowy Owl
numbered '1.34.', and inscribed
pencil and watercolour, heightened with white and gum arabic
21⅜ x 14½ in. (54.3 x 36.9 cm.)
London, 4 October 1994, £34,500 ($54,510)
Record auction price for a watercolour by the artist

John Gould (1804-1881), ornithologist, writer and publisher produced a monumental series of illustrated books of birds throughout the world, *The Birds of Great Britain* being his most successful. The Godman collection of 230 original watercolours for this publication was sold in October 1994 and realised £1.03 million ($1.6 million). This was the largest group of Gould watercolours ever seen at auction.

Opening the sale and bringing the highest prices were a number of watercolours of birds of prey by Joseph Wolf. Wolf was highly regarded as a wildlife artist of considerable reputation as well as a natural history illustrator. In 1849 Landseer predicted of him: 'When a good many artists of the present generation are forgotten, Wolf will be remembered.'

MARIAN ELLIS ROWAN (1848-1922)
Twenty-two Butterflies, all of the Nymphalidae family
signed 'Ellis Rowan'
watercolour with bodycolour on grey paper
22⅛ x 13¼ in. (56.2 x 33.7 cm.), one sheet from a set of three
Sold in aid of the Merlin Trust
London, 16 May 1995, £20,700 ($32,436)

Born and raised in Victoria, Ellis Rowan inherited a keen interest in flora and fauna from her father Henry Ryan, who created one of Australia's great gardens at Derriweit on the slopes of Mount Macedon, and from her grandfather John Cotton, an amateur naturalist and ornithologist who had published books on English birds in the 1830s and emigrated with his family to Australia in 1843. This watercolour was one of several painted in New Guinea in 1917-18 toward the end of Ellis Rowan's prolific career. These were subsequently inherited by Merlin Montagu Douglas Scott, her great-nephew, and were sold to raise funds for the Merlin Trust, a charity set up to sponsor the work of young horticulturists and commemorating Merlin Scott, an avid naturalist killed in action in North Africa in 1941, and his father Sir David Montagu Douglas Scott, Ellis Rowan's nephew.

The thirty-six sheets depicting insects, mostly Lepidoptera (butterflies and moths), from the island of New Guinea sold for a total of £206,885 ($324,809).

EDWARD ROBERT HUGHES, R.W.S. (1851-1914)
Midsummer Eve
signed 'E.R. Hughes. RWS.'
watercolour heightened with bodycolour on paper
45 x 30 in. (114.3 x 76.2 cm.)
New York, 15 February 1995, $464,500 (£295,860)
Record auction price for a work by the artist

E.R. Hughes was the nephew of the Pre-Raphaelite painter Arthur Hughes and acted as studio assistant to William Holman Hunt, helping him to complete the version of *The Light of the World* in St. Paul's Cathedral when the master's sight was failing. He specialised in painting imaginative and literary themes in watercolour, exhibiting regularly with the Royal Watercolour Society, of which he became Vice-President.

*Midsummer Eve*, which he exhibited at the R.W.S. in 1908, is one of his most attractive and romantic pictures. There are echoes of the work of the poet and novelist George MacDonald, whom the artist and his uncle both knew well; E.R. Hughes had been engaged to his daughter Mary before her death in 1878. In its imagery and supernatural subject, the picture anticipates the well known *Night with her Train of Stars* (1912; Birmingham City Art Gallery). However, while *Night* is a sombre, symbolist theme, set in the sky, *Midsummer Eve* is terrestrial and playful.

# VICTORIAN PICTURES

JOHN WILLIAM WATERHOUSE, R.A. (1849-1917)
The Crystal Ball
signed and dated 'J.W. Waterhouse 1902'
oil on canvas
47½ x 31 in. (120.7 x 78.7 cm.)
London, 4 November 1994, £221,500 ($358,830)

Exhibited at the Royal Academy in 1902, the picture originally showed a skull on the table, emphasising the idea that the model represents a sorceress in her cell. A later owner, presumably finding the detail distasteful, had it painted out, but it was uncovered during restoration after the sale, greatly adding to the picture's composition and narrative force.

*Top:*
ARTHUR HUGHES (1832-1915)
Ophelia
signed 'Arthur Hughes' and inscribed 'Put heads in sky/and more
leaves/purple' under the mount
oil on panel
20 x 36 in. (50.8 x 91.4 cm.)
London, 4 November 1994, £595,500 ($964,710)
Record auction price for a work by the artist

WALTER FIELD (1837-1901)
Henley Regatta
signed and dated 'W. Field 1884'
oil on canvas
55 x 95¼ in. (139.7 x 242 cm.)
London, 4 November 1994, £135,700 ($219,834)
Record auction price for a work by the artist

SIR EDWARD COLEY BURNE-JONES, Bt., A.R.A. (1833-1898)
Portrait of Frances Graham
signed with initials and dated 1879
oil on canvas
23½ x 17½ in. (59.7 x 44.5 cm.)
London, 10 March 1995, £177,500 ($285,775)

Frances was the fourth child of William Graham, a wealthy India merchant and Member of Parliament for Glasgow, who was Burne-Jones' greatest patron. She herself became a close friend of the artist, and was the most important of the young women with whom he enjoyed romantic but platonic relationships in later life.

This haunting portrait, painted in 1879 when she was twenty-one, is his only formal likeness of her, although she appears in several of his subject pictures; it is contemporary with the famous 'Orpheus' piano (private collection) which he designed and decorated for her use. In the 1880s, by then married to Sir John Horner and living at Mells Park in Somerset, Frances became a leading member of the coterie known as 'The Souls'. She was to include a long account of Burne-Jones in her memoirs *Time Remembered* (1935).

Burne-Jones' portrait of Frances' daughter Cicely, painted fourteen years later than her mother's and in the same family collection until the 1970s, was sold by Christie's in London on 9 June 1995 for £122,500.

SIR LAWRENCE ALMA-TADEMA, R.A. (1836-1912)
The Finding of Moses
signed and dated 'L Alma Tadema/OP.CCCLXXVII'
oil on canvas
53¾ x 84 in. (136.7 x 213.4 cm.)
New York, 25 May 1995, $2,752,500 (£1,713,132)
Record auction price for a work by the artist

On 10 December 1902 the great dam at Aswan was opened by the Duke of Connaught. The event, observed the *Illustrated London News*, marked 'a new epoch in the history of the Nile', while for the British contractor, Sir John Aird, it crowned a career which had brought him a baronetcy, a seat in Parliament, and the means to form a magnificent collection of modern academic pictures. One of the finest of these was Alma-Tadema's sumptuous if sinister *Roses of Heliogabalus* (1888), which Christie's auctioned in 1993 for the record price of £1,651,500. Aird invited the artist to attend the ceremonies at Aswan (a fellow guest was the young Winston Churchill, fresh from his Boer War triumphs), and Alma-Tadema offered to paint *The Finding of Moses* – another great event which had occurred on the Nile – to mark the occasion.

The result was the undisputed masterpiece of his last decade, a period which, characteristically, saw no decline in the work of this most professional of artists. He treated the well-known story in *Exodus* with a good deal of freedom, notably in showing Pharoah's daughter taking the infant home instead of handing him over to his mother and sister for rearing. The eye is seduced by one of his most scintillating colour schemes, the brilliant blues and purples of the larkspurs and the lotus flowers being set off by scattered touches of orange, yellow and pink.

But neither artistic licence nor aesthetic imperatives undermine the

archaeological accuracy for which the artist was famous. Cartouches on the princess's throne identify her as the daughter of Ramses II (1279-1212 B.C.), who is generally assumed to be the Pharoah of the Exodus. The party is approaching Memphis, the capital of the Old Kingdom, probably making for the temple of Ptah, the god of creation, whose priests, their ritually shaven heads and fine white linen drapery signifying purification, figure prominently in the entourage. The bound Asiatic captives represented on the princess' footstool refer to the Israelite captivity, while on the far bank, against a backdrop of the Pyramids of Gizeh, droves of Hebrew slaves labour under the watchful eyes of swarthy Egyptian overseers. Memphis and Gizeh are indeed close, both being near the modern Cairo. Aswan is many miles up-river.

The picture offers a dramatic index of the vicissitudes of taste. When it was exhibited at the Royal Academy in 1905, the reaction against Victorian narrative painting had already begun, and critical response was muted. Alma-Tadema had been paid 5,000 guineas, but the picture fetched only 260 guineas when the executors of Sir Jeremiah Colman sold it in 1942. The nadir of its fortunes was reached in 1960, when Newman's, the London dealers, were unable to sell it or even to find a museum to take it as a gift.

But its star, never seen to full advantage and lately ignominiously eclipsed, was soon to rise to new and dizzy heights. As critics have often pointed out, Alma-Tadema's true artistic legacy lies not in painting but in the products of the epic film industry, blockbusters such as Cecil B. De Mille's *Cleopatra* (1934) and *The Ten Commandments* (1956), the script-writers and designers for which are known to have studied his work. It was therefore appropriate that in the late 1960s, when the Victorian revival was well under way, *The Finding of Moses* should go to New York, enter the great Alma-Tadema collection formed by Allen Funt, the man behind the 'candid camera', and in 1973 be exhibited with the rest of the collection at the Metropolitan Museum itself. In the world of American entertainment the picture had found its spiritual home and long-delayed apotheosis. It has never looked back.

CASPAR DAVID FRIEDRICH (German, 1774-1840)
Fischerboot zwischen Findlingen am Ostseestrand
oil on canvas
8⅝ x 12¼ in. (22 x 31.2 cm.)
London, 13 October 1994, £639,500 ($1,010,410)

Friedrich's *Fischerboot zwischen Findlingen am Ostseestrand* can be placed among a group of paintings of evening and night seascapes from the early 1830s. This group was produced during a resurgence of creative activity in the work of the artist after a period of relative stagnation caused by illness. His increased expectation of death led to a new and subtle symbolism, emphasized by a heightened sensitivity towards the representation of light and a greater understanding of colour. The approaching boat represents forthcoming death, while the figures observe it and contemplate the closeness of the end of life. They are positioned between two large pointed monoliths which pierce the sky and demonstrate strength of faith before the gradually brightening horizon, which opens to the afterworld. In contrast with the naturalistic colour theories of his contemporaries, such as Göethe, Friedrich exaggerated the properties of light and colour, true to his Romantic ideal.

His exceptional ability to 'use' nature for his iconography was described by C.A.Nilson in 1833: 'His paintings are hieroglyphs of nature, whose specific states are highlighted by the artist, by transferring his own thoughts and states on corresponding representations of nature.' It was, however, in the eyes of some contemporaries, exaggerated and was frequently criticised as distortion of the beauty of nature in its pure form.

The artist's *Mondacht am Strand mit Fischen* of circa 1816-18 (Schloss Charlottenburg, Berlin) may be viewed as a forerunner to this work, with its formal arrangement of subject matter, limiting the spectator's view of the middle ground. Iconographically, however, it is not a direct predecessor. The picture can also be compared with *Mondaufgang am Meer* of circa 1822 (Nationalgalerie, Berlin, Wagenersche Sammlung, no.53) in which figures, seated on a large monolith, watch boats approach against a light horizon. While similar in subject matter and colour range, however, this picture evokes a deeper mysticism through vaguer brushwork and outline. The final and mature development of these symbols appears in *Die Lebenstufen* of circa 1835 (Museum der Bildenden Künste, Leipzig, inv.no.1217), in which Friedrich and his family represent three Stages in Life, he himself facing the approaching ships and, hence, his forthcoming death.

Few paintings by Friedrich appear on the open market, but Christie's have sold two others in the last ten years. *Winterlandschaft* (bought by the National Gallery, London) and *Spaziergang in der Abenddämmerung* (bought by the J. Paul Getty Museum, California).

*Top:*
JOHANN PHILIPP EDUARD GAERTNER
(German, 1801-1877)
Unter den Linden, Berlin
signed with initials and dated 'EG/1836'
oil on canvas, 8½ x 16 in. (21.5 x 40.5 cm.)
London, 13 October 1994, £243,500 ($384,730)

ANDRIES SCHELFHOUT (1787-1870)
A Winter Landscape
signed and dated 'A. Schelfhout 1848'
oil on panel
27 x 38¼ in. (68.5 x 97.5 cm.)
Amsterdam, 26 April 1995, Fl.644,000 (£259,677)
Record auction price for a work by the artist

*Above:*
JEAN-FRANÇOIS MILLET (French, 1814-1875)
The Sower (Le Semeur)
signed 'J. F. Millet'
pastel and black crayon on pale brown paper
14⅞ x 16⅞ in. (36 x 43 cm.)
New York, 15 February 1995, $882,500 (£562,102)

*Right:*
CONSTANT TROYON (French, 1810-1865)
The Ferry Crossing
signed and dated 'C. TROYON./1849.'
oil on canvas laid down on board
45¾ x 62 in. (116.2 x 157.5 cm.)
New York, 25 May 1995, $497,500 (£312,893)

CHARLES-FRANÇOIS DAUBIGNY (French, 1817-1878)
Un Village près de Bonnières
signed and dated 'Daubigny 1861'
oil on canvas
33½ x 59 in. (85 x 150 cm.)
New York, 25 May 1995, $354,500 (£222,956)
Record auction price for a work by the artist

JAMES JACQUES JOSEPH
TISSOT (French, 1836-1902)
Mavourneen,
Portrait of Kathleen Newton
signed and dated 'J. J. Tissot/1877'
oil on canvas
35¾ x 20 in. (88.2 x 50.8 cm.)
New York, 25 May 1995,
$2,532,500 (£1,592,942)

*Mavourneen* is one of Tissot's earliest
portraits of Kathleen Newton, the
beautiful young woman who captured
his heart, and provided his inspiration
for the decade they shared together
before she died from consumption at
the age of 28.

*Mavourneen* is also one of Tissot's
most exquisite depictions of the
'ravissante irlandaise', as Kathleen
Newton was often called. It is
elegant in its simplicity. Tissot
emphasizes her beauty and strong
silhouette by placing her against a
soft white shade, thereby creating
a study of contrasts between the
velvety blacks of her stylish coat
and wide-brimmed hat, and the
gentle light that shines through
the window. Tissot's etching after
*Mavourneen* was the most popular of
his prints; it was exhibited with
other portraits of Kathleen Newton
at the Grosvenor Gallery in 1878.
The title of the painting and print
was based on a popular Victorian love
song, *Kathleen Mavourneen*, meaning
'my darling' or 'my dear one'. The
lyrics describe two lovers who will
be parted and sadly foretells the
tragic final chapter of one of the
greatest Victorian love affairs – that
of James Tissot and Kathleen Newton.

JACQUES-EMILE BLANCHE
(French, 1861-1942)
Vaslav Nijinsky in Michel Fokine's
*Danse Siamoise*, from the
divertisement *Les Orientales*, or
*Le Baiser Sacramentel de l'Idole*
signed 'J.E. Blanche'
oil on canvas
86½ x 47¼ in. (220 x 120 cm.)
New York, 25 May 1995,
$662,500 (£416,667)

Jacques-Emile Blanche was, with
Pierre Bonnard, Kees Van Dongen
and Léon Bakst among the first artists
to paint dancers from 'Les Ballets
Russes'. In the tradition of Manet
and Degas, Blanche prepared this
portrait of Nijinsky from photographs. As the artist was unable to
convince the dancer to pose in his
studio, he invited Eugène Druet,
accompanied by Auguste Rodin, in
June 1910, to photograph Nijinsky
in his salon and garden at Auteuil.
Nijinsky, in his second season with
Diaghilev's ballet in Paris, was, in
Bakst's words, 'L'Idole du Public'; he
was known by students of the
Academy of Beaux Arts as 'Dieu de
la Dance'. The artist's *chef d'oeuvre*
perfectly represents the dancer's spirit
through the exuberant arrogance of
his stylized pose, and accordingly, he
christened the work *Le Baiser
sacramentel de l'Idole.* The painting
was previously on loan to the
Theatre Museum, London.

FREDERICK ARTHUR BRIDGMAN (American, 1847-1928)
Day of the Prophet at Oued-el-Kebir
signed and inscribed 'F.A.Bridgman/Fête de Oued-el-
Kebir/Blidah/Algerie'
oil on canvas
59⅝ x 78⅞ in. (151.5 x 200.4 cm.)
London, 17 November 1994, £551,500 ($865,855)
Record auction price for a work by the artist

A pupil of Gérôme, Bridgman travelled several times to Egypt and Algeria in the 1870s and 1880s. Although very much more an outsider, Frederick Arthur Bridgman was always inquisitive about aspects of Algerian life usually unseen by Europeans. On one of his winter stays, he went to Blida on the feast of the Mouloud, the birthday of the Prophet Mohammed. The ritual slaughtering of sheep was followed by the frenzied dancing of members of the Assaonias sect; by evening, several thousand people had arrived at the Oued-el-Kebir cemetery and the little mosque was filled to overflowing. 'The cold blue-white tombs and gravestones now in deep shade,' wrote Bridgman, 'the hundreds of long tapers lighted in anticipation of the night procession, the glowing fires of the cafés under the long sweeping olive-boughs, formed an ensemble of colour and mystery that seemed quite unreal.' His thick hair, which had hidden his European clothes, slipped off, and feeling in danger, he beat a retreat, leaving the crowd to spend the night in conversation, praying and singing. That night must have made a vivid impression on him, for the spirituality and conviviality of the feast are strongly expressed in this oil. *The Day of the Prophet at Oued-el-Kebir* was one of Bridgman's major exhibition paintings shown at the height of his career.

GUSTAV BAUERNFEIND (German, 1848-1904)
At the Entrance to the Temple Mount, Jerusalem
signed and dated 'G. Bauernfeind/Jerusalem 1886'
oil on canvas, 61¼ x 48⅝ in. (155.5 x 123.5 cm.)
London, 17 November 1994, £375,500 ($589,535)
Record auction price for a work by the artist

# IMPRESSIONIST AND MODERN PICTURES

## *AN IMPRESSIONIST MASTERPIECE STIRS THE MARKET*

*by Jussi Pylkkänen*

The celebrated Danish collector Wilhelm Hansen, most of whose pictures are in the Museum at Ordrupgaard outside Copenhagen, was the first owner of Monet's *Cathédrale de Rouen, Effet d'Après-midi.* An impressionist collector of excellent taste, Hansen had a sophisticated eye for the best French paintings of the period. Drawn to the Bernheim-Jeune gallery in Paris by his unquenchable thirst for the leading impressionists, Hansen was unable to resist what he already then recognised as a masterpiece of modern painting. There is little doubt that this was an impulse buy driven by passion more than by reason. Worried by his wife's reaction to his purchases on what was to have been an ordinary business trip, Hansen wrote an apologetic letter home:

'By the way, I used my spare time to look at paintings and I may as well admit now instead of later, that I have been impulsive and have made a sizable purchase. I know though that I will be forgiven when you see what I have bought; it is all first class with star rating. I have bought Sisley (two wonderful landscapes), Pissarro (a lovely landscape), and a Claude Monet (*La Cathédrale de Rouen*), one of his most famous works' (letter of 22 September 1916).

Hansen had bought one of Monet's masterpieces. Some eighty years later the beauty and importance of the painting has lost none of its currency. Collectors travelled from all over the world to view it and the competition for the picture began some months before the sale. Rarely have we experienced such a charged atmosphere and intense bidding battle at Christie's, as the painting raced to £7.59 million – the highest price paid for a modern painting at auction in Europe in recent years.

*Effet d'Après-midi* belongs to a series of thirty paintings of Rouen Cathedral executed by Monet in a period of intense activity between 1892 and 1894. The work of a mature artist at the peak of his powers, the vast majority are now in museum collections. Other versions have found their way into the Museum of Fine Arts, Boston, the Folkwang Museum, Essen, the Schlossmuseum, Weimar and the Musée d'Orsay, Paris. Interestingly the Musée d'Orsay owns the sister-piece to the present painting which Joachim Pissarro suggests was also painted between February and April 1892. Both are painted in this striking blue and catch the cathedral façade just after noon as the sun is at its strongest and the contours of the cathedral at their most expressive. These are, after all, entirely abstract works where expression is far more important than subject. Herein lies their ultimate quality. Art transcends life as Monet presents us with a monumental, breathtaking painting of an essentially dull, lifeless subject.

Their quality owes much to Monet's intensity and to the hours that he spent working and reworking the surface of the paintings. Although the series was begun in 1892, Monet refused to exhibit any of the paintings until the whole series was finished. Indeed, he would often return to apparently finished works to make adjustments and improvements. Each painting was begun *en place*, in front of the cathedral before it was moved to his studio in Giverny for completion. All thirty *Cathédrales* were begun and finished in this way before Monet was satisfied enough with the results to put his signature to each painting. Over the years of hard work his attachment to the paintings had become so strong that when they were eventually exhibited at Durand-Ruel in 1894, Monet still entertained the idea that they would be bought as a group for the nation.

The response to the 1894 exhibition was remarkable. Critics, the public and fellow artists alike rose as one to pay tribute to Monet's extraordinary achievement. Pissarro wrote of Monet's 'maîtrise extraordinaire', Signac praised his virtuosity and Berthe Morisot simply exclaimed 'elles sont magnifiques'.

In the same year Monet offered for sale several works from the series. These were sold through Durand-Ruel for the extremely high price of Fr.15,000 each. Monet was clearly reluctant to part with his masterpieces. The present painting is a fine example of this: considered by Monet among the best of the whole series, it remained with him for twenty years before being sold.

Few pictures can truly be called masterpieces of modern painting and these appear even more rarely on the market. Therefore, one hundred years on, it came as little surprise that the painting was met with such excitement and universal praise.

*Right:*
CLAUDE MONET (French, 1840-1926)
La Cathédrale de Rouen, Effet d'Après-midi (Le Portail, plein Soleil)
signed and dated 'Claude Monet 94'
oil on canvas
41¾ x 28¾ in. (106 x 73 cm.)
London, 26 June 1995, £7,591,500 ($12,138,808)

HENRI DE TOULOUSE-LAUTREC (French, 1864-1901)
Danseuse ajustant son Maillot (Le premier Maillot)
signed 'H T Lautrec'
oil on board
23¼ x 18¼ in. (59 x 46.5 cm.)
New York, 9 November 1994, $4,787,500 (£2,992,180)

# *TOULOUSE-LAUTREC'S* LE PREMIER MAILLOT *AND MONET'S* NYMPHEAS

## *by Michael Findlay*

Stunted and misshapen though he was, Henri de Toulouse-Lautrec enjoyed both the high and the low-life of *fin-de-siècle* Paris as much as any cavalry officer. Born into a minor aristocratic family, his deformity and his vocation thrust him into the *demi-monde* of louche dance halls and brothels where he wielded his brush and palette as both a social critic, a voluptuary and an empathizer. Disdaining the orthodoxy of academic genre painting, most of the group that became known as the Impressionists took to the fields and attempted fidelity to Nature. Having had enough of country life as a child, Toulouse-Lautrec decided that the ballet, the circus and the cabarets of Montmartre would provide him his subject matter.

Although some of his works record the actual performances of singers and *vaudevillians*, his most penetrating paintings present us with the poignancy of the entertainer (acrobat or prostitute) at an off-moment: in preparation before the curtain rises or, perhaps exhausted, after the show. *Danseuse ajustant son Maillot (Le premier Maillot)* epitomizes his genius at catching his subject, not only unawares, but lost in a world of their own imagining. As the title suggests, this charming young lady is so young as to have just finished dressing as a dancer for the very first time. She stands with her tutu tucked under her chin adjusting the new pink tights she has pulled up over her long coltish legs, perhaps just a little bit nervous about her debut. She is completely unaware of our prying eyes, devoid of self-consciousness; yet we imagine that we can read her thoughts. The private reverie of this would-be opera 'rat' (as the trainee dancers were called) becomes a frozen moment of silent poetry enhanced rather than diminished by the bareness of her environment. Concentrating on an oblique form and with the merest whisper of paint indicating floor and walls, Toulouse-Lautrec gives the greatest form and substance to the object of her gaze, the bright pink tights and ballet shoes. Though down-turned, he reveals to us her pretty snub-nosed face, hair escaping from a bun and her long arm that matches her lanky legs. With equal substantiality he might have also rendered her frothy tutu, but instead he merely intimates it in quick sure strokes of line and colour (mostly white), un-bothered by the *pentimenti* which almost suggests motion as she ruffles the skirt up and it spills behind her, looking like nothing so much as wings, further enhancing the angelic nature of this child-woman.

Unlike many of the Impressionists, Monet in particular, who commenced an image while out of doors but laboured (often for months, if not years) to complete it in the studio, Toulouse-Lautrec provides us with a vision which is created from start to finish *in situ*. His editing out of extraneous information is unabashed yet subtle and his emphasis exquisite. We look at *Danseuse ajustant son Maillot (Le premier Maillot)* and even across the divide of a hundred years we need not struggle to grasp the meaning or understand the method – we are there and it is now.

Stubbornly claiming an addiction to being able to paint only what he actually saw and affecting a journeyman attitude towards his calling, Monet was in fact one of the first painters to bear witness to an essentially spiritual cognisance that was recognised (by

Kandinsky, in particular) as the prelude to the advent of an abstract art. In his series of grain stacks and of Rouen Cathedral (see pp. 52-3) in the 1890s he allowed the light to dissolve the details of his subjects to the point of near-invisibility so that form and colour reigned virtually supreme. Even then, however, he presented his structures in an orthodox manner seen head-on against a horizon.

This changed dramatically when he constructed his water garden at Giverny in 1893, little knowing that it would provide him with a vision that would compel him for the rest of his life, over a quarter of a century. As he began to cultivate and control his lily-pond, he found not only a universe within but that it was the perfect mirror, literally and figuratively, for what he claimed to be his only real subject matter – light and the weather. *Nymphéas* is one of 48 paintings of his water garden that Monet finally exhibited at Durand-Ruel Galleries in Paris in May of 1909, and to thundering applause. He had been working on the series since 1900 and never considered exhibiting anything but the group, as a whole. Although universally admired for their colour, skill and delicacy few at the time understood quite how revolutionary were these voluptuous waterscapes. One critic, however, quickly grasped the great difference between these works and virtually the entire tradition of Western painting, a tradition that Monet had now altered ineradicably:

'M. Claude Monet has painted the surface of the pond in a Japanese garden where water lilies bloom; but he has painted only this surface, seen in perspective, and no horizon is given to these paintings, which have no beginning or end other than the limits of the frame, but which the imagination extends as far as it likes.' (A. Alexandre, *Le Figaro*, 7 May 1909.)

Thus was established the hegemony on the field of colour used and abused by artists throughout the twentieth century, and perhaps without this breaking of the code by Monet, we might have had no Kandinsky, no Klee and no Miró and certainly no Pollock and no Rothko. With just four canvases, Monet went even further than 'the limits of the frame' and created tondos, our *Nymphéas* being the only one of these not in a major museum. Strikingly unusual although not without precedent, these suggest a limitless sea of colour as if the canvas represents the pupil of the artist's roving eye. This painting is particularly subtle as it glows with the warmth of the lily blossoms gently floating on the sheer stillness of the impenetrable water.

Maligned as a late twentieth-century movement, 'minimalism' is still the key to understanding the essential differences between Western art of the nineteenth century and that of our times. Consider the Toulouse-Lautrec's *Danseuse ajustant son Maillot (Le premier Maillot)*, stripped of all references save those absolutely essential to the private drama we are privileged to witness. He eschews virtually all 'detail', such detail as would make us admire the excellence of an Ingres or even a David ('look, you can even see the reflection in the pearls'). Equally so Monet's *Nymphéas* where the artist seems to have magnified a mote and there is nothing 'happening', no trees, no people, no town, just the pared down examination of a sheet of water with some floating flora.

CLAUDE MONET (French, 1840-1926)
Nymphéas
signed and dated 'Claude Monet 1907'
oil on canvas
31¼ in. (79.5 cm.) diameter
Sold from the collection of Alice Tully
New York, 9 November 1994, $3,302,500 (£2,064,063)

CAMILLE PISSARRO (French, 1830-1903)
La Récolte des Foins à Eragny
signed and dated 'C Pissarro 1887'
oil on canvas
20 x 26 in. (51 x 66 cm.)
London, 28 November 1994, £1,013,500 ($1,582,073)

*La Récolte des Foins à Eragny* is among Pissarro's most striking works of the 1880s. Painted in the summer of 1887 it dates from a year when he executed only ten paintings. This was doubtless due to the rigours of the new *pointilliste* technique with which Pissarro had recently begun to experiment. In doing so he was following the lead of Georges Seurat and Paul Signac who had introduced him to their methods in 1885. While theirs was a relatively studied and static technique, Pissarro introduced a more flowing comma shaped stroke to the *pointilliste* vocabulary which gave his work a liveliness more reminiscent of his early *plein-air* paintings. Above all Pissarro gave *pointillisme* a luminosity which it had never had before. *La Récolte* is a fine example of this.

VINCENT VAN GOGH (Dutch, 1853-1890)
Jeune Homme à la Casquette
oil on canvas
18¾ x 15⅜ in. (47.5 x 39 cm.)
New York, 11 May 1995, $13,202,500 (£8,356,013)

At no time in his short ten-year career as an artist did van Gogh subject the portrait to such ambitious scrutiny as during the summer and autumn of 1888 when he was living in Arles. As he wrote in a letter of 3 September to his brother Theo:
'I want to paint men and women with that something of the eternal which the halo used to symbolize, and which we seek to convey by the actual radiance and vibration of our colouring... Ah, the portrait, the portrait with the thought and the soul of the model in it, that is what I think must come.'

In *Jeune Homme à la Casquette*, van Gogh painted an unknown gamin easing into adolescent bravura. Impassively nonchalant, perhaps even sullenly defiant, this concentrated image of early manhood has a distinctly 'modern' ring.

ODILON REDON (French, 1840-1916)
Bouquet de Fleurs
signed 'Odilon Redon'
oil on canvas
25¾ x 19⅞ in. (65.4 x 50.4 cm.)
Sold from the collection of Dian Woodner and Andrea Woodner
Amsterdam, 7 December 1994, Fl.1,265,000 (£460,000)

After the turn of the century, Redon increasingly turned to flower pieces. They were executed in pastel or oil and attracted considerable public and critical attention. Even during his lifetime, they became a hallmark for his art. When working in the more enduring medium of oil, he was striving for a decorative effect that was as luminous and opaque as his pastels. This flowerpiece, that dates from about 1905, is an example of Redon's striving for a pastel-like effect in oil. It is one of the rare unvarnished pieces, and the background with its hues of pink, purple and brown creates a dreamlike atmosphere. The flowers themselves, however, are realistic and can easily be identified: mostly anemones in different hues and states of flowering.

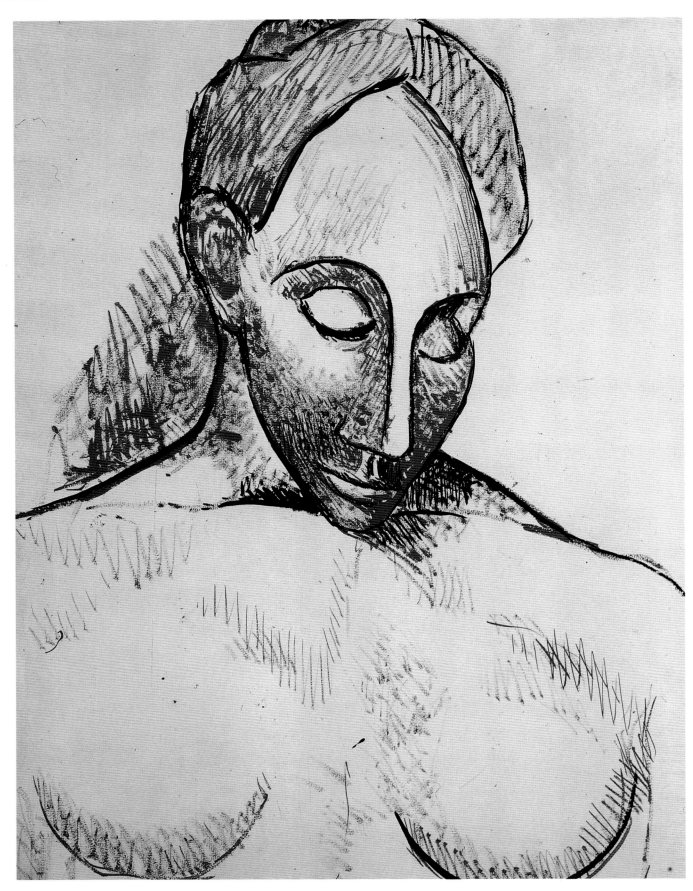

PABLO PICASSO (Spanish, 1881-1973)
Tête de Femme
signed in red crayon 'Picasso'
red gouache and brush and black ink on Ingres laid paper
24¾ x 18⅞ in. (63 x 48 cm.)
Sold from the collection of Mr. Gustav Zumsteg, Zurich
London, 26 June 1995, £1,761,500 ($2,816,638)

When Picasso painted *Tête de Femme* in 1906, a number of influences
were at work which would eventually combine to produce one of the
icons of modern art *Les Demoiselles d'Avignon* two years later. Strongest
among these influences was undoubtedly his study of primitive and
ancient Iberian art, which in its sculpture had a finesse of line and
form which greatly belied its apparent simplicity. In this simplicity
was a native purity which Picasso wanted to bring to modern
painting. Hence he cast aside his fine modelling and sinuous line of
the pink and blue periods in favour of an abstraction based on line
and volume which would lead naturally to *Les Demoiselles
d'Avignon* of 1907. *Tête de Femme* is one of the largest and most
striking works on paper produced by Picasso during this period.

PABLO PICASSO (Spanish, 1881-1973)
Mère et Enfant
signed and dated 'Picasso 22'
oil on canvas, 39½ x 32 in. (100.5 x 81.5 cm.)
Sold from the collection of The Honorable Pamela Harriman
New York, 11 May 1995, $11,992,500 (£7,590,190)

According to Christian Zervos, this painting was completed in 1922, five years after Picasso travelled to Rome and met Olga Khoklova, a dancer whom he married the following year. In February, 1921, Olga bore Picasso a son, Paulo, and for the next few years, the theme of motherhood and childhood was featured in many of Picasso's major paintings.

Initially, the theme was inextricable from the monumental figures which Picasso had been painting since his trip to Rome. The tenderness and plentitude that are part and parcel of these gigantic mothers and their massive offspring lingers on in *Mère et Enfant*, though the style in which they are presented shifts toward something far more lyrical and delicate, almost ethereal.

Interestingly enough, however, no less an authority on the work of Picasso than William Rubin has compellingly and conclusively refuted the notion that this is an image of Olga Picasso with her son Paulo, arguing instead that it is a portrait of the Picasso family's close friend Sara Murphy. For all of its gentility and graceful melancholy, then, Picasso's icon of motherhood contains within it the subversive strain that is the bedrock of Picasso's great work.

PABLO PICASSO (Spanish, 1881-1973)
Tête de Femme
signed, inscribed and dated 'Picasso Fontainebleau Septembre 1921'
pastel on grey paper
25½ x 19⅞ in. (64.8 x 50.5 cm.)
London, 28 November 1994, £2,091,500 ($3,264,831)

Picasso's classical figure drawings of the 1920s are among his most striking and successful works on paper. This particular example was previously in the celebrated collection of Billy Wilder and relates closely to a whole series of pastels executed in the same year as the monumental oil *Trois Femmes à la Fontaine*, now in the Museum of Modern Art, New York.

AMEDEO MODIGLIANI (Italian, 1884-1920)
Nu assis au collier
signed 'Modigliani'
oil on canvas, 36 x 23½ in. (91.5 x 59.7 cm.)
Sold from the collection of Mr. and Mrs. Ralph F. Colin
New York, 10 May 1995, $12,432,500 (£7,819,182)

*Nu assis au collier* is from the second series of nudes which Modigliani executed in 1917, one of three portraits of an unnamed model. The paintings of nude women which Modigliani completed the year before, in 1916, express an odd combination of languor and disjointedness, self-conscious about their debt to both classicism and primitivism. In *Nu assis au collier*, these dissident influences have been poetically resolved in favour of an unabashed sensuality (these are no longer *masques*, but 'real' naked women), heightened by an enveloping purity rarely evident in Western Art since the Renaissance. In every respect, this work embodies the totality of Modigliani's vision as an artist.

JOAN MIRÓ (Spanish, 1893-1983)
La Table (Nature Morte au Lapin)
signed and dated 'Miró 1920'
oil on canvas, 51¼ x 43⅜ in. (130 x 110.5 cm.)
Sold from the collection of Mr. Gustav Zumsteg, Zurich
London, 26 June 1995, £4,731,500 ($7,565,668)

Painted in 1920 *La Table* is one of the most important of all early works by Miró. Its sister piece, *Table au Gant,* is in the Museum of Modern Art in New York. *La Table* was painted immediately after Miró's first visit to Paris. There he had met many of the great *avant-garde* Cubist French painters, including André Masson and Picasso. Picasso was quick to recognise Miró's obvious talent, introducing him to many influential friends and buying an early self-portrait from him. Honoured though he doubtless was, the young Catalan refused to succumb to such apparent flattery, returning home to proclaim: 'The French (and Picasso) are doomed because they have an easy road and they paint to sell'.

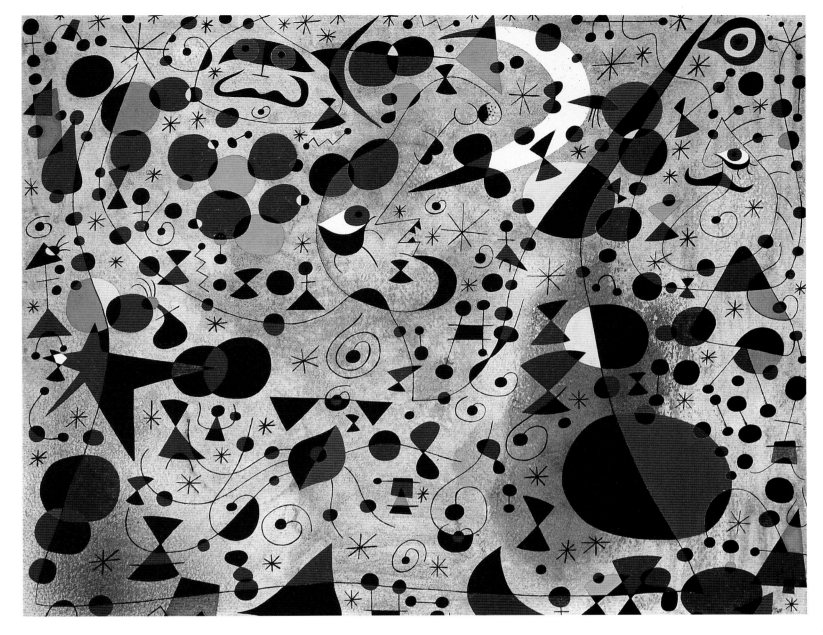

JOAN MIRÓ (Spanish, 1893-1983)
La Poétesse
signed 'Miro', signed again and titled on the reverse 'Joan Miró
31.XII.1940, La Poétesse Palma de majorque'
gouache and oil wash on paper
15 x 18 in. (38 x 46 cm.)
Sold from the collection of Mr. and Mrs. Ralph F. Colin
New York, 10 May 1995, $4,732,500 (£2,976,415)

Miró's *La Poétesse* belongs to an exquisite series of twenty-three gouaches collectively known as the *Constellations*. This complete cycle of creativity, related in size, medium, and imagery (sun, stars, birds, lovers), was for the artist the culmination of a period of intense withdrawal due to the outbreak of World War II. Miró painted *La Poétesse*, the fourteenth constellation, while living in complete isolation in Palma de Mallorca.

*La Poétesse* is one of the most poetic and lyrical of the *Constellations*. In it, Miró created a delicate and vast cosmic network of intersecting black lines and richly coloured shapes. The entire surface is bathed in nocturnal light and mobilized with darting lines which define figures and stars. An additional layer of intense flashes of colour gives the impression of sparks in the night. The *Constellations* symbolized for Miró a rebirth of faith in man's role in the cosmic order after the 'dark night'.

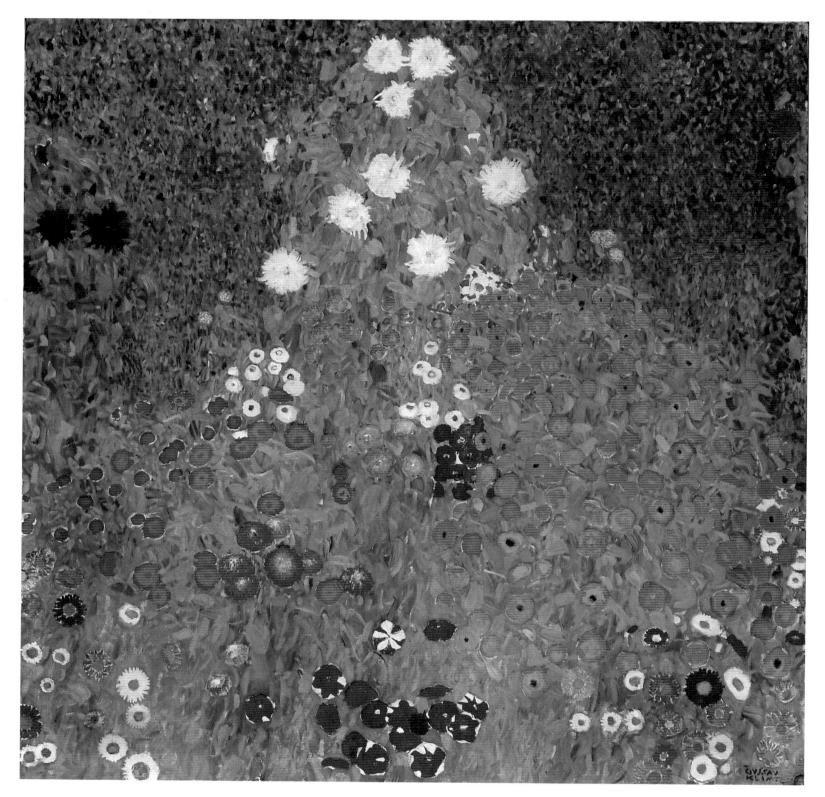

GUSTAV KLIMT (Austrian, 1862-1918)
Bauerngarten (Blumengarten)
signed 'Gustav Klimt'
oil on canvas
43¼ x 43¼ in. (110 x 110 cm.)
London, 28 November 1994, £3,741,500 ($5,840,481)

Known principally as a fine figurative painter, Klimt only began to
paint landscapes in the late 1890s. In addition to being supremely
decorative and vibrant in colour, the best of these are compositionally
complex and match the mystery of his finest portraits.

*Right:*
KARL SCHMIDT-ROTTLUFF (German, 1884-1976)
Einfahrt
signed and dated 'S-Rottluff 1910'
oil on canvas
30¼ x 33½ in. (77 x 85 cm.)
London, 13 October 1994, £958,500 ($1,514,430)

LOVIS CORINTH (German, 1858-1925)
Eisbahn im Berliner Tiergarten
signed and dated '1909 Lovis Corinth'
oil on canvas
25¼ x 35⅞ in. (64 x 90 cm.)
London, 13 October 1994, £364,500 ($575,910)

ERNST LUDWIG KIRCHNER
(German, 1880-1938)
Liegende
hand-painted carved wood (chestnut)
27 in. (68.5 cm.) long
London, 13 October 1994,
£276,500 ($436,870)

*Right:*
EMIL NOLDE (German, 1867-1956)
Dampfer im Sonnenuntergang
signed 'Nolde'
watercolour on Japan paper
13⅛ x 17¾ in. (33.2 x 45.2 cm.)
London, 13 October 1994,
£177,500 ($280,450)

MANÉ-KATZ (French, 1894-1962)
Les Musiciens (quartet)
signed 'Mané-Katz'
oil on canvas
39⅜ x 31⅞ in. (100 x 81 cm.)
Tel Aviv, 25 September 1994,
$140,000 (£87,538)

SIR JOHN LAVERY, R.A., R.S.A., R.H.A. (1856-1941)
On the Loing
signed and dated 'J. Lavery 1884'
oil on canvas
31 x 30 in. (79 x 76 cm.)
London, 22 November 1994, £293,000 ($466,000)
Record auction price for a work by the artist

A larger version *On the Loing: An Afternoon Chat* (*Under the Cherry Tree*), is in the collection of the Ulster Museum, Belfast. Lavery had planned the larger painting, now considered to be the thesis statement of his *plein air* painting style of this period, on this canvas. It was painted at Grez-sur-Loing during 1884 and celebrates the peaceful, rustic community dominated by the River Loing.

GWEN JOHN (1876-1939)
A Corner of the Artist's Room in Paris
(with open Window)
oil on canvas laid on board
12½ x 10 in. (31.8 x 25.4 cm.)
London, 20 June 1995, £122,500 ($196,000)

An extremely rare and interesting interior by Gwen John, this work greatly exceeded its pre-sale estimate, and was one of the highlights of the summer sale. The work was painted on the top floor at 87 rue du Cherche-Midi, Paris. Gwen John moved there in March 1907 and stayed until 1909. The table and basket-work chair are familiar props from this period, and can also be seen in *The Convalescent* series of paintings of a young girl from the 1920s.

*Above:*
LAURENCE STEPHEN LOWRY, R.A.
(1887-1976)
Punch and Judy
signed and dated 'L.S.Lowry 1943'
oil on canvas
16 x 22 in. (40.6 x 55.8 cm.)
Sold from the collection of
The Reverend Geoffrey Bennett
London, 23 March 1995,
£152,200 ($242,000)

LAURENCE STEPHEN LOWRY, R.A.
(1887-1976)
Cowles Fish & Chips, Cleator Moor
signed and dated 'L.S.Lowry 1948'
pastel on green paper
10¾ x 14½ in. (27.3 x 36.8 cm.)
Sold from the collection of
The Reverend Geoffrey Bennett
London, 23 March 1995, £45,500 ($72,300)
Record auction price for a pastel by the artist

*Above:*
GRAHAM SUTHERLAND, O.M.
(1903-1980)
Standing Form, Red Background
(against Curtain)
signed and dated 'Sutherland 1949'
oil on canvas
57⅞ x 26⅜ in. (147 x 67 cm.)
London, 26 October 1994,
£73,000 ($119,700)

*Top right:*
PETER BLAKE, R.A. (b.1932)
Pin-Up Girl
cryla on board
11½ x 9½ in. (29.3 x 24.2 cm.)
Sold from the collection of the late
Rt. Hon. Lord Grimond of Firth
London, 26 May 1995,
£12,650 ($20,360)

*Above:*
DAME BARBARA HEPWORTH
(1903-1975)
Garden Sculpture (Meridian)
signed, dated and numbered
'Barbara Hepworth 1958 6/6'
bronze with a pale and dark green patina
66 in. (168 cm.) high
London, 26 October 1994,
£89,500 ($146,800)

*Left:*
GIOVANNI GIACOMETTI (1868-1933)
Herbstmorgen (Stampa), 1908
signed with monogram 'G.G.'
oil on canvas
25⅝ x 27½ in. (65.5 x 70 cm.)
Zurich, 10 April 1995, S.Fr.464,700 (£246,291)
Record price for a painting by the artist

*Below left:*
ERNEST BIÉLER (1863-1948)
Sur le Chemin de l'Église, 1904
signed 'E. Biéler'
oil on canvas
45¼ x 62¾ in. (115 x 157 cm.)
Zurich, 10 April 1995, S.Fr.430,800 (£228,324)
Record price for a painting by the artist

*Right, clockwise from top left:*
JOSE HONORATO LOZANO
(Philippine, c.1815-c.1885)
Manila and its Environs; an album of
twenty-five watercolours depicting scenes in
and around Manila
(*Mestizos en trage de fiesta* illustrated)
twenty-one signed 'Jose Honorato Lozano',
one signed 'Jose Hozano', two signed
'Jose H. Lozano' and one signed 'Jose Lozano'
watercolour and bodycolour
each sheet 9¾ x 13½ in. (24.7 x 34.3 cm.) or
13½ x 9¾ in. (34.3 x 24.7 cm.)
Sold from the collection of M. Jean Flebus
London, 14 July 1995, £265,500 ($421,879)

WILHELM AUGUST RUDOLF
LEHMANN (German, 1819-1905)
Portrait of Captain Sir Richard Francis Burton
oil on canvas
36 x 28 in. (91.5 x 71.1 cm.)
Sold from the collection of the Lord Talbot
of Malahide, removed from Wardour Castle
London, 14 July 1995, £111,500 ($177,173)

ERNEST ALFRED HARDOUIN
(French, 1820-1854)
Het Koningsplein, Batavia
(Lampangan Merdeka, Gambir, Jakarta)
oil on canvas
29 x 56¼ in. (73.5 x 143 cm.)
Amsterdam, 25 April 1995, Fl.241,500 (£99,383)

# AUSTRALIAN PICTURES

*Above:*
JOHN GLOVER (1767-1849)
A View between the Swan River and King George's Sound
oil on canvas
20 x 28 in. (51 x 71 cm.)
Melbourne, 4 April 1995, A.$ 387,500 (£175,976)

*Right:*
WILLIAM STRUTT (1825-1915)
Equestrian Portrait of two Members of the Victorian
Mounted Police in Bush Dress (one of a pair)
signed and dated 'W Strutt 1861'
oil on canvas
15 x 14 in. (38.5 x 36 cm.)
Melbourne, 6 December 1994, A.$184,000 (£90,999)

ARTHUR MERRIC BLOOMFIELD BOYD (born 1920)
Bride Drinking from a Pool
signed 'Arthur Boyd'
tempera on composition board
51 x 60 in. (129.5 x 152.5 cm.)
Melbourne, 4 April 1995, A.$156,500 (£71,072)

# AMERICAN PICTURES

*Top:*
THOMAS MORAN (1837-1926)
The Cliffs of Green River, Wyoming
signed and dated 'T Moran 1881'
oil on canvas
25 x 65 in. (64.8 x 158 cm.)
New York, 30 November 1994, $2,752,500 (£1,761,600)

THOMAS BIRCH (1779-1851)
View on the Delaware
signed 'T Birch'
oil on canvas
27 x 39 in. (68.5 x 99 cm.)
New York, 22 September 1994, $107,000 (£67,410)

*Top:*

CHARLES COURTNEY CURRAN (1861-1942)
Tangled Vines
signed and dated 'Charles C. Curran, N.A. 1919'
oil on canvas, 24¼ x 36⅛ in. (61.4 x 91.8 cm.)
New York, 16 March 1995, $112,500 (£69,750)

FREDERICK CARL FRIESEKE (1874-1939)
Garden in June
signed 'F.C. Frieseke'
oil on canvas, 25⅛ x 32 in. (63.7 x 81.2 cm.)
New York, 24 May 1995, $937,500 (£600,000)

# LATIN AMERICAN PICTURES

DIEGO RIVERA (Mexican, 1886-1957)
Naturaleza Muerta con Flores, Escudilla de Fruta,
Libro y Tarro de Jengibre
signed and dated 'D.M.Rivera II-18'
oil on canvas
28⅜ x 36⅜ in. (72 x 92.5 cm.)
New York, 16 May 1995, $1,487,500 (£953,526)
Record auction price for a work by the artist

This still life is a transitional and experimental post-Cubist work executed by Rivera in his Paris studio in February 1918. The Mexican master had been living and working in Paris since he moved from his native Mexico in 1911. During the First World War, he was a leading member of the Cubist circle of Picasso, Gris, Lipchitz, Gleizes, Metzinger, and other French and emigré artists. At the end of 1917, Rivera abruptly left his classical cubist style and began an intensive period of research and assimilation of the late style and palette of Paul Cézanne. This particular painting of February 1918, unusually large for this period, is one of Rivera's most emphatically Cézannian works, to the point that it can be considered an obvious homage to Cézanne.

This still life is unusual within the development of Rivera's post-Cubist 1918-19 *oeuvre*, primarily because of its size. It is most probably a unique experimental work, in which Rivera tentatively returns to semi-naturalistic forms evoking and treating several well-known Cézannian clichés, such as the deliberately arranged still life setting, the distinctively 'French' motifs (*pot à crème*, floral patterned wall-paper, ginger jar, book, fruit bowl, and patterned ceramic flower vase). What makes the work so particularly and overtly Cézannian, and in that sense unique among Rivera's still lifes of the period, is the disposition of the broadly unfolding and heavily patterned textile cloth, bulky in its weight, which cascades in voluminous folds over the carefully wrought (in paint) wooden table-top.

JOAQUIN TORRES-GARCIA (Uruguayan, 1874-1949)
Composition symétrique universelle en blanc et noir
signed and dated 'J Torres Garcia 31'
oil on canvas
48 x 24¾ in. (122 x 63 cm.)
New York, 16 May 1995, $937,500 (£600,962)
Record auction price for a work by the artist

1931 represented a significant year for the development of Torres-García's constructivism, and the artist summed this up well in a letter to his friend, the Spanish writer and critic Guillermo de Torre:

'When I am able, I will show you through photographs and other reproductions. It's something of a style that could be called 'cathedral'. Something strong, very mature (the synthesis of all my work), very just, in a constructive sense, and even better, something new because it is the most ancient, the prehistoric, as Lipschitz asserts. I am satisfied because of this and also because, in the final analysis, I have had total recognition here.'

ROY LICHTENSTEIN (American, b. 1923)
Kiss II
signed and dated 'rf Lichtenstein '62'
oil on canvas
57⅛ x 67¾ in. (145 x 172 cm.)
New York, 3 May 1995, $2,532,500 (£1,544,825)

By 1962 several young artists in New York were using discredited media images – from advertising, comic books, billboards, and television – as sources for their art. When Roy Lichtenstein had his first solo exhibition of comic book paintings at the Leo Castelli Gallery that year, he was joined forever in the eyes of the public with the other so-called Pop artists – Oldenburg, Warhol, Rosenquist, Wesselmann, Segal – a group whose impact is still being felt today. 'In the notorious marriage of a wholly radical subject matter with the methods of fine art, Roy Lichtenstein brought to a level of consciousness, both visual and intellectual, an awareness of the American lifestyle and brilliantly proclaimed the comic strip as a fitting theme for the new American painting of the 1960s.' (D. Waldman, *Roy Lichtenstein*, New York, 1969, p.12.) Just as Warhol used images appropriated from fan magazines and movie publicity stills to create his iconic images of American Pop culture of the 60s – Marilyn, Elvis, Liz – so too did Lichtenstein create

'stereotypes of our culture – a Hollywood sunset, a crying girl, an embracing couple' from the lowly comic book.

*Kiss II* is a magnificent example of Lichtenstein's early comic book style. His refinement of all of the 'fine art' elements of the picture – sensuous line, strong composition, bold flat areas of colour – give this representational painting all the impact of a contemporary abstraction. What appears to be a simple quotation of a commercial comic artist's work has become, through Lichtenstein's masterful intervention, the equivalent in artistic terms of Picasso or Matisse, precise and bold.

ANDY WARHOL (American, 1930-1987)
Shot Red Marilyn
signed, dedicated and dated 'ANDY WARHOL/64'
synthetic polymer and silkscreen inks on canvas
40 x 40 in. (101.6 x 101.6 cm.)
New York, 2 November 1994, $3,632,500 (£2,422,000)

Although Warhol had used images of movie stars such as Troy Donahue in his early paintings, it was his series of portraits of Marilyn Monroe, begun shortly after her death in 1962, which are the most memorable of all his works of the period. Warhol utilizes a studio publicity photograph of the actress that portrayed her at the beginning of her rise to fame in the national consciousness, which defined her as a glamorous sex symbol. This is what caught Warhol's immediate attention in addition to the amount of publicity her suicide was receiving in the press. However, Marilyn's troubled life and death by suicide betrayed the surface gloss of glamour and revealed the seamier side of celebrity, something which Warhol was just discovering for himself in his own rapid ascent to fame. Marilyn, as Warhol portrayed her, thus became one of the most powerful icons of the tragic celebrity, whose glamorous life could not protect her from the harsher realities of real life.

The technique used for *Shot Red Marilyn* created the most striking images of his series of Marilyns. Warhol would hand paint the canvas with coloured shapes corresponding to Marilyn's face. 'Creating in effect a coloured map of her face, he first laid down a yellow patch for hair, blue for shadow, red for lips, flesh tone for face and green for collar ... Then, after the paint had dried, he placed the silkscreen over the canvas and squeezed black pigment through the mesh, thereby superimposing the photographic image with the coloured ground.' (D. Bourdon, *Andy Warhol*, New York, 1989, pp. 124-5.)

*Shot Red Marilyn* was created out of an incident that occurred at Warhol's first Factory on East 47th Street in 1964:

'The Factory's clouded reputation as a kind of amoral free zone where anything could happen attained a new peak one autumn day in 1964 when Dorothy Pedber ... visited the place ... Pedber walked to the front of the Factory, where Warhol had leaned several forty-inch-square *Marilyn Monroe* portraits against the wall, slowly took off a pair of white gloves, reached into her purse, pulled out a pistol, and aimed at the movie star's forehead, shooting a hole through the entire stack. Then she returned the gun to her purse, put on her gloves, and smiled triumphantly in Warhol's direction before departing on the elevator. It was the first time anyone had fired a gun in the Factory, and Andy was visibly upset. But he had the canvases repaired and they subsequently became known as The Shot Marilyns.' (*Ibid.*, p. 190.)

FRANCIS BACON (British, 1902-1992)
Study for a Portrait: 1952
oil on canvas
26 x 22 in. (66 x 56 cm.)
London, 29 June 1995, £793,500 ($1,253,730)

Painted during the most important year of Bacon's early career, *Study for a Portrait* is an icon of twentieth-century neuroses.

As with the artist's contemporaneous paintings of screaming Popes, it depicts a man of high office – a politician, businessman or dictator – reduced to his loneliest and most naked self. Enclosed in the suffocating void of an isolation chamber, he gives vent to his angst and pain with a primal wail that creates a black hole for a mouth. Not since Edvard Munch's *The Scream* have such nihilistic despair and mental anguish been so convincingly communicated.

YVES KLEIN (French, 1928-1962)
La Grande Bataille (ANT 103), 1961
blue pigment on paper laid down on canvas
113 x 146 in. (286 x 371 cm.)
London, 29 June 1995, £947,500 ($1,497,050)

In the late 1950s the French artist Yves Klein invented one of the most controversial painterly techniques in the lexicon of post-war art history. At his direction and often in front of a large invited audience, his female models would cover their naked bodies with blue paint and press themselves against sheets of white paper. The resulting imprints were called 'anthropometries' and exemplified the artist's desire to distance himself from the creation of his work.

*La Grande Bataille* is the largest and most important of Klein's 'anthropometries' ever to come to auction. One of the few body paintings to which he gave a title, the overall composition suggests that a judo match (Klein was a judo expert) has been held in a blue mud bath.

ASGER JORN (Danish, 1914-1973)
Allegretto Furbo
signed and dated 'Jorn 64', oil on canvas
63¾ x 51⅛ in. (162 x 130 cm.)
London, 29 June 1995, £188,500 ($297,830)

*Top:*

ANSELM KIEFFER (German, b. 1945)
Die Königin von Saba am Strand von Juda
titled, 1983-6
oil, acrylic, emulsion and shellac on canvas with metal wires and lead
70⅞ x 173¼ in. (180 x 440 cm.)
London, 29 June 1995, £485,500 ($767,090)
Record auction price for a work by the artist

PIERRE ALECHINSKY (Belgian, b. 1927)
Le Passé inaperçu
signed and dated 'Alechinsky/1981'
acrylic and india ink on paper laid down on canvas
81 x 185 in. (206 x 470 cm.)
London, 29 June 1995, £199,500 ($315,210)
Now in the Pompidou Centre, Paris

ISAMU NOGUCHI (American, 1904-1989)
Sun
marble
54 x 54 x 24 in. (137.2 x 137.2 x 61 cm.)
Sold from the collection of the Museum of Modern Art
Corporation from the Estate of Nina Bunshaft, sold to benefit
the Nina and Gordon Bunshaft Fund for acquisitions in the
Department of Painting and Sculpture
New York, 3 May 1995, $552,500 (£337,025)

Carved in brilliant white marble, this version of Isamu Noguchi's
*Sun* was executed at the time of collaboration between the artist
and the renowned International-Style architect Gordon Bunshaft
on the sculpture garden of the Beinecke Rare Book and
Manuscript Library at Yale University. The theme of *Sun,* with its
inherently powerful connotations, would occupy Noguchi from
1959 until 1969, leading to the creation of two of his most
important and beautiful public sculptures: a version at the Beinecke
Library (1960-64), and the monumental granite *Black Sun* (1969) at
the Seattle Art Museum.

Noguchi created this rare work specifically for Bunshaft and
endowed it with the mystery and cosmic energy of a life-force. The
work alludes to the power of the sun in the artist's 'representation
of the infinite, the formless state of life and matter which is the
basis of all being ... [Noguchi] consciously creates forms that are,
in a sense, 'inhabited' and inescapably associative rather than
purely abstract and non-referential.' (S. Hunter, *Isamu Noguchi,*
New York, 1978, p.153.)

GERMAINE RICHIER (French, 1904-1959)
La Mante Grande
bronze
height excluding base, 51⅛ in. (130 cm.)
Sold from the collection of Chris and Lucila Engels, Curaçao
London, 1 December 1994, £210,500 ($329,643)

The grotesque mutation of a woman and a giant praying mantis, this sculpture is perhaps the most famous of the monstrous forms created by Richier to convey the brutality of occupied Europe. Here the standard war-time image of woman as nurturing mother or dutiful daughter has been corrupted. In its place Richier creates an aggressive *femme fatale* whose gaunt body seems barren and decomposed by its belligerence and cannibalism.

As one of the few female artists to achieve fame prior to the women's liberation movement of the 1960s, Richier has been lauded as a proto-feminist. As such, *La Mante Grande* has come to be interpreted as a symbol of female supremacy.

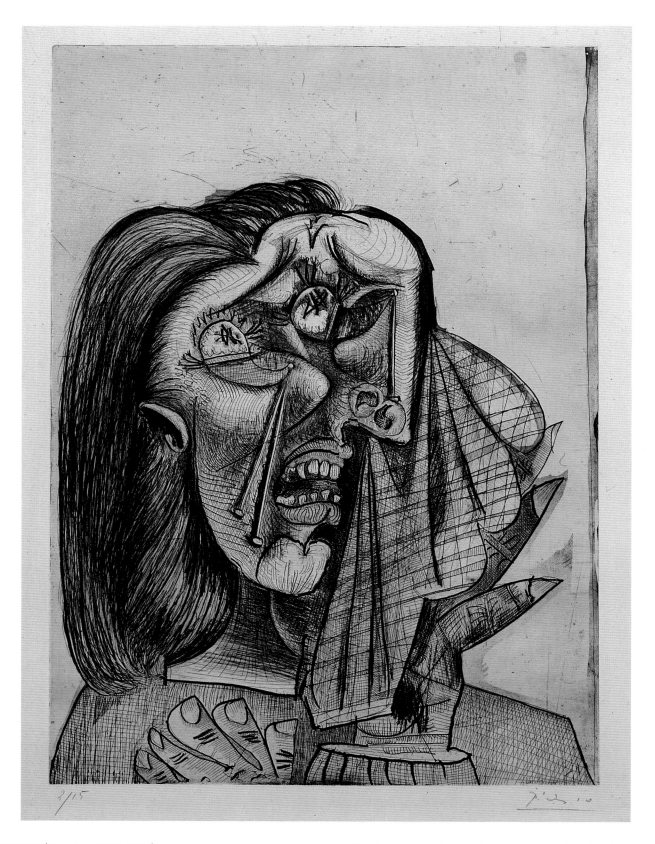

PABLO PICASSO (Spanish, 1881-1973)
La Femme qui pleure, I (Bloch 1333)
etching, 1937, a fine impression of this very rare print
signed in pencil, numbered 2/15
P. 27⅜ x 19⁹⁄₁₆ in. (69.5 x 49.7 cm.)
New York, 18 November 1994, $1,036,500 (£660,191)
Record price for a print sold at auction in America
Now in the collection of The Art Institute of Chicago

On 1 July 1937, less than one month after his final work on *Guernica*, Picasso began work on the plate which was to become *La Femme qui pleure, I.*

The theme of the Weeping Woman was one which had occupied the artist for several months. Between January and June 1937 he had produced the pair of etchings *Sueño y Mentira di Franco* (Bloch 297-8) in which the woman first appears, screaming at the sky, a comment on the horrors of the Civil War in Spain.

Working feverishly on the plate the artist took this through seven states, producing editions of 15 in the third and in this, the seventh and final state.

*Top:*

HENRI MATISSE (French, 1869-1954)
HENRI MATISSE, *Jazz*, Tériade, Paris, 1947 (Duthuit 22)
pochoirs from the edition of 250
overall S. 17½ x 13½ in. (44.5 x 34.2 cm.)
Donated by Madame Alice Tériade and sold to benefit L'Institut
Gustave-Roussy, Villejuif for Cancer Research
London, 30 June 1995, £95,000 ($151,050)

MARC CHAGALL (Russian, 1887-1985)
LONGUS, *Daphnis et Chloé*, Tériade, Paris, 1961
(Mourlot 308-349)
lithographs, from the edition of 250
overall S. 16½ x 12½ in. (42 x 32 cm.)
Sold from the collection of Dr. Sali Guggenheim
London, 2 May 1995, £133,500 ($214,935)

*Left:*
MAURICE BRAZIL PRENDERGAST (American, 1859-1924)
Figures in the Park (Clark, Mathews and Owens 1664)
monotype in colours with additions in graphite and coloured pencils,
circa 1895-7, signed in the plate
S. 15⅛ x 11 in. (38.4 x 28 cm.)
New York, 9 May 1995, $244,500 (£153,774)
Record price for a print by the artist

JASPER JOHNS (American, b. 1930)
Flag
screenprint in colours, 1973, signed in pencil, a unique trial proof for the right
side of *Flags I* (Field 173)
S. 27⅛ x 18⅝ in. (69 x 47.5 cm.)
New York, 10 May 1995, $123,500 (£77,673)

WASSILY KANDINSKY (Russian, 1866-1944)
Der Spiegel (Roethel 49)
linocut in colours, 1907
L. 12⅝ x 6¼ in. (32 x 16 cm.)
Formerly in the collection of Mr. and Mrs. Robert S. Benjamin
New York, 10 May 1995, $145,500 (£91,509)

# REFLECTIONS OF EUROPE:
## WHISTLERS FROM AN AMERICAN COLLECTION

## *by Anne Spink*

One of the most famous commercial transactions in the annals of American print collecting was negotiated in 1919 between Howard Mansfield, a New York lawyer, and Harris Whittemore, a Connecticut industrialist. Mansfield sold his entire collection of some six hundred etchings and lithographs by James McNeill Whistler – exceptional impressions carefully selected over a period of forty years – for $350,000. The sale made newspaper headlines. At the time, a *New York Sun* reporter quoted Mansfield as saying '... if $1,000,000 were given to anyone with which to duplicate the collection it could not be done.'

On 9 May 1995, Christie's New York auction results confirmed Mansfield's comments regarding the intrinsic monetary value of his Whistler prints and again called public attention to impressions of a quality the world's finest museums would be proud to own. Fifteen etchings from the original Mansfield group were consigned by Harris Whittemore's descendants and realised a total of nearly $300,000 – a sum not far from that paid for all six hundred impressions earlier in the century.

Mansfield was seventy years old and his eyesight failing when he sold his Whistler prints to Whittemore; he had spent more than half his life actively collecting them. By 1890 he had begun a trans-Atlantic correspondence with Whistler, receiving news of the artist's latest projects and arranging to visit him in London and Paris. Whistler advised Mansfield about which of his finest and rarest proofs to acquire. As a testament to the importance of their friendship – and certainly proof of the artist's marketing skills – Whistler inscribed some of his proofs to Mansfield. Such was the case with *The Palaces* (M.184: K.187) which sold for $13,800 in the May sale. Ultimately the supreme quality of his collection indicates that along with the intelligence and tenacity to seek Whistler's guidance, Mansfield also possessed the eye and enthusiasm of a dedicated connoisseur. In addition to the collection itself, Mansfield's other contributions include his authorship of the first descriptive catalogue *raisonné* of Whistler etchings to be published in America and the formulative influence he had on the buying taste of compatriots like museum founder Charles L. Freer.

By the 1890s Harris Whittemore was already building one of America's finest private collections of paintings by the European Impressionists, Mary Cassatt and Whistler, once owning the latter's celebrated *Symphony in White, No 1: The White Girl* and *Mother of Pearl and Silver: The Andalusian*. In 1985, eleven of the Whittemore's Impressionist paintings formed the basis of an important single-owner sale at Christie's. Over the years Whittemore also acquired outstanding etchings by Cassatt, Pissarro, Rembrandt and McBey. Most of these prints were dispersed around 1950. In 1983, through a private transaction, the Whittemore family sold all of their Whistler lithographs. These are now on deposit at The Art Institute of Chicago and will be the basis of a forthcoming catalogue *raisonné*.

The Mansfield/Whittemore Whistler etchings auctioned by Christie's were exceptional in many ways. Six were impressions cited in both Mansfield's and the now more standard, illustrated catalogue *raisonné* by Edward G. Kennedy; several were subjects from Whistler's two highly successful Venetian sets created in 1879-80 (including two dramatically different states of *Nocturne* (M.181; K.184); other images, such as *The Embroidered Curtain* (M.411; K.410) from the etching series done in Amsterdam in 1889, exist in very few impressions.

The most extraordinary print in the group was a unique working proof of the first state of *Sunflowers, Rue des Beaux-Arts* (M.417; K.422) extensively touched in ink and annotated by Whistler. Its selling price of $81,700 established a new world record for a Whistler etching at auction and underscored the consistently high quality of this collection which Fritz Lugt aptly classified as 'l'une des meilleures qui soient, et qui peut être classée la deuxième ou la troisième du monde.'

JAMES McNEILL WHISTLER
(American, 1834-1903)
Sunflowers, Rue des Beaux-Arts (M.417; K.422)
etching extensively touched in ink, circa 1892-3,
signed with the butterfly and inscribed 'imp' in pencil
8¾ x 11 in. (22.2 x 27.9 cm.)
Sold from the collection of the
Harris Whittemore Jr. Trust
New York, 9 May 1995, $81,700 (£51,471)
Record auction price for an etching by the artist

# SCULPTURE

ANTONIO SUSINI (Italian, active 1580-1624)
A Pair of bronze Figures of Angels
late 16th Century
7¾ in. (9.25 cm.) high, 8⅛ in. (20.5 cm.) high
New York, 26 October 1994, $657,000 (£595,000)

These two angels belong to a series of six that formerly decorated the hexagonal marble tabernacle of the Holy Sacrament behind the high altar of the Certosa di Galluzzo, just south of Florence.

Another of the series is in the National Gallery of Australia in Canberra. The sculptural decoration was completed by a statuette of the Risen Christ in the Metropolitan Museum, New York, and by Four Evangelists, three of which are known. Archival documents record that in 1596 Giambologna received a total payment of 215 lire via his foundryman, Antonio Susini.

Although various of the figures are closely based on prototypes by Giambologna, his biographer Baldinucci, who was generally well-informed, records that he delegated responsibility for the tabernacle to Antonio Susini.

A Venetian rock crystal Ewer
13th or 14th Century
11 in. (28 cm.) high
London, 13 December 1994,
£199,500 ($311,220)

This is the second largest surviving medieval rock crystal ewer, and one of fewer than forty now known. Although such objects are not easy to place or date precisely, the bold simplicity of the present piece suggests that it is among the earliest of the type, and that it was probably executed in Venice during the fourteenth century.

GOTTFRIED TURAU
(German, active early 18th Century)
A carved ivory Table Cabinet
signed 'Gotfr. Turau invenit et fecit'
first quarter 18th Century
15⅛ x 11 x 6¼ in. (38.4 x 27.9 x 15.8 cm.)
London, 13 December 1994,
£89,500 ($139,620)

The present cabinet, which is one of the few signed works by Gottfried Turau, represents a major addition to understanding of his artistic achievement. Best known for his collaboration on the legendary Amber Room, and for other works in amber, Turau must now also be recognised as a highly accomplished ivory-carver.

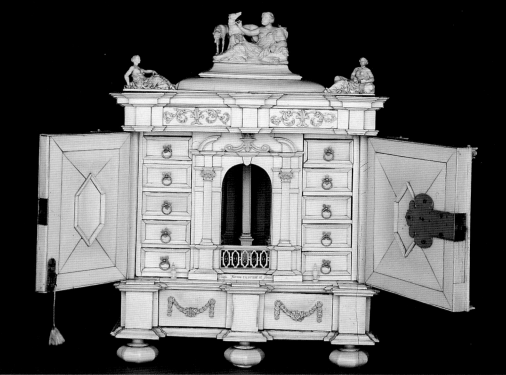

COADE & SEALY (British, 1769-1820)
A Coade stone Sundial tripod Pedestal
inscribed 'COADE & SEALY/LONDON'
early 19th Century
12 in. (30.5 cm.) diameter; 44 in. (112 cm.) high
Wrotham Park, 13 June 1995, £19,996 ($31,994)

RICHARD JAMES WYATT (British, 1795-1850)
A white marble Figure of a Huntress
signed 'R. J. WYATT Fecit/ROMAE'
60½ in. (153.6 cm.) high
London, 3 November 1994, £67,500 ($109,350)

PROFESSORE GIOLLI (Italian, late 19th Century)
A white marble Figure of a Girl
signed 'Prof. Giolli/Galleria P. Barzanti Florence'
the figure, 54¼ in. (138 cm.) high
the pedestal, 34½ in. (87.6 cm.) high
London, 2 March 1995, £73,000 ($115,851)

WILLIAM COUPER (American, 1853-1942)
'Coming of Spring', a marble Figure
signed 'Wm Couper' and inscribed 'Florence'
81 in. (205.7 cm.) high
Sold from the Estate of Tom D. White
New York, 24 May 1995, $96,000 (£54,720)

# WORKS OF ART FROM HOUGHTON

## by Charles Cator

The Houghton sale was an extraordinary event and it has rightly taken its place in the history of fabled auction sales. Why is it that some sales capture the imagination of the collecting world and remain enshrined in the minds of later generations? Names like San Donato, Hamilton Palace, Almina, Countess of Carnarvon, Percival Griffiths – all echo with a resonance that defies the years. Their attraction has retained its force, not just historically and aesthetically, but also in very real financial terms. Any interested outsider who was not actually part of the furniture world, would be amazed to discover that the Percival Griffiths sale, constantly referred to with as much excitement and reverence as if it had taken place a few years ago, was in fact held at Christie's in May 1939. Such is the power of these sales to capture the imagination of the collecting world. They are perceived to be great events in their time and so they remain in the eyes of future generations.

Of course the essential requisite for any great sale must be superb works of art and on this it will be continuously judged. Yet quality alone, however brilliant, cannot ensure that magic. So many other associations surround a work of art – the circumstances of its commissioning and subsequent history, whether it has remained with one family or passed through many different hands, the whole story of how it has been acquired, admired, loved, neglected, coveted, abandoned throughout its existence. This spirit that has moved others in the past, however humble, is quintessential to any work of art and becomes an integral part of its beauty.

Few groups of objects could have had a more romantic provenance than those from Houghton, nor been appreciated and loved by a more remarkable series of owners. The combined inheritance of four great families: Walpole, Cholmondeley, Rothschild and Sassoon had created an extraordinarily rich and diverse collection, from which objects were selected for the sale only after long and careful consideration of their suitability for display at Houghton.

The principal part of the sale was made up of works of art from the collection of Sir Philip Sassoon, Bt. (1888-1939) whose sister, Sybil Sassoon, married the Earl of Rocksavage, later 5th Marquess of Cholmondeley, in 1913. Sir Philip's legendary taste was brilliantly evoked by James Knox in his essay *Sir Philip Sassoon, Bt., Aesthete, Collector, Patron.* The extent and range of his eclectic and highly informed connoisseurship was unparalleled, encompassing the modern classical interiors and magnificent gardens of Port Lympne, the sumptuous French eighteenth-century paintings and decorative arts, some inherited from the Parisian *hôtel* of his Rothschild grandparents, Baron and Baronne Gustave, which enriched the beautiful rooms of his London house, 25 Park Lane, as well as the restrained Queen Anne and early Georgian walnut and lacquer furniture, needlework, silver and English conversation-pieces with which he filled the perfectly understood rooms of Trent Park, the country house not far from London that he completely remodelled in 1925.

After his early death in 1939, his sister inherited the majority of his collections and these were assimilated into Houghton, some by way of Lady Cholmondeley's London house, 12 Kensington Palace Gardens which she gave up in 1979.

By no means all of Sir Philip's multifaceted collection has left Houghton and careful thought was given to retaining works of art that complement the interiors of Houghton. Many of the English conversation pictures remain and the chinoiserie gilt and lacquer pieces from Trent (including a superb pair of hanging cabinets acquired by Sir Philip from nearby Raynham Hall) form a particularly happy addition to the Cabinet Room, rehung with Chinese wallpaper by the 3rd Earl of Orford following the sale of his grandfather's picture collection to Catherine the Great.

The magic of so many of Sir Philip's objects lay in their combination of great quality with the charm of rich but mellow materials – patinated gilt-bronze, polychrome lacquer and sumptuous old silk velvets and needlework. In fact they evoked the very *douceur de vivre* that is so charmingly captured in one of Sir Philip's most distinguished purchases – *La Lecture*

JOSEPH BAUMHAUER (French, *maître* 1749) and JEAN-FRANÇOIS LELEU (*maître* 1764)
A Louis XVI brass-inlaid ebony *Meuble d'Appui*
stamped once '★JOSEPH★', twice 'J.F.LELEU' and once 'JME'
63¾ in. (162 cm.) wide; 37 in. (94 cm.) high; 19¾ in. (50 cm.) deep.
London, 8 December 1994, £903,500 ($1,409,460)

de Molière by Jean-François de Troy (p. 7) – which he had the foresight to buy as early as 1919. The group of Louis XV and Louis XVI lacquer and *vernis Martin* with its emphasis on green demonstrated so perfectly his preference for the unusual but understated. The green lacquer was complemented by the distinctive group of ormolu-mounted green porcelain vases. Their restrained elegance was balanced by the robust character of the three magnificent pairs of blue porcelain vases, with their bold early neo-classical mounts.

The researches of our consultant, Patrick Leperlier, yielded some interesting new provenances. The splendid mantel clock by Charles Cressent with its semi-circular dial was identified in the sale in 1771 of Louis-Antoine Crozat, baron de Thiers. In the nineteenth century it belonged to Lady Cholmondeley's grand-parents and is recorded at 23, avenue Marigny in a watercolour by Eugène Lami, dated 1882. The most exciting addition to furniture research was perhaps the discovery of the stamp of Joseph Baumhauer on the *meuble d'appui*, which was originally part of the *coquillier* commissioned by Lalive de Jully. This confirmed the attribution to Joseph of Lalive's remarkable suite of neo-classical furniture, the earliest in the *goût grec* style. Patrick Leperlier also unravelled more of the complex subsequent history of Lalive's *coquillier*, showing how it had been acquired with Lalive's *hôtel* in rue Ménard by the maréchal de Choiseul-Stainville, who then had it remodelled by Jean-François Leleu for his new house in the rue d'Artois.

There could have been no more eloquent representation of the heights achieved by English craftsmen in the early eighteenth century than the six pairs of chairs from Sir Robert Walpole's Houghton. The perfect balance of line and profile that these chairs display is equal, if not superior, to anything created in the rest of Europe at the time. The two main suites from Houghton, the walnut and parcel-gilt set, probably originally supplied for the earlier house, and the satyr-mask set have both been partially displaced since the late eighteenth century, as a result of the redecoration of the Cabinet Room and the White (formerly Green Velvet) Drawing Room following the sale of the pictures. Since then it has never been possible to display them in their entirety. Similarly the introduction in the early nineteenth century of the Cannons Suite to the Marble Parlour led to its original eagle chairs

being moved to the Yellow Drawing Room which in turn meant that the walnut 'Yellow Caffey' suite from there had to be relocated. Of course these changes were all part of the continuing evolution of a great house and it is exciting that in the last years of the twentieth century, Lord Cholmondeley intends to return the majority of the State Rooms to their appearance recorded in the inventory taken after Sir Robert's death in 1745. It is possible to do this because as John Cornforth, who knows and understands Houghton better than anyone, pointed out in his essay *The Creation of Houghton*, apart from Sir Robert's plate and pictures, almost everything else from his time survives in the house.

The highlights of the sale were exhibited in New York in October and Paris in November before the main London viewing in the first week of December. Against a specially designed backdrop of enlarged black and white photographs of Houghton, 25 Park Lane and Trent Park, the pictures, furniture, silver (pp. 130-1)and precious objects sparkled like jewels. It was exciting to see them each time afresh, undimmed by re-acquaintance, and fascinating to be able to examine and discuss them anew. Through all these conversations across the world in which I learnt so much about these objects I had grown to love, I always found myself reflecting on the great and noble house from which they had come, standing with complete confidence in its broad and gentle park, so grand and yet so simple – surely the greatest work of art of them all, whose future has been secured by this sale.

*Above:*
ENNEMOND-ALEXANDRE PETITOT (French, 1727-1801)
A Pair of Louis XV porphyry and gilt-bronze two-handled Vases
16¼ in. (41.5 cm.) wide; 15¼ in. (39 cm.) high; 11 in. (28 cm.) deep
London, 8 December 1994, £1,926,500 ($3,005,340)

Petitot was responsible for bringing neo-classicism to Parma, where he worked for his patron Philip, Duke of Parma. Petitot's design for these vases is one of thirty plates engraved by Benigo Bossi (1727-1792) in Parma in 1784 and dedicated to Guillaume-Léon du Tillet, marquis de Felino (1711-1774), the Prime Minister of Parma. Another pair of vases is in the J. Paul Getty Museum, California.

Attributed to the ROBERTS family
A Pair of George I burr-walnut and parcel-gilt Side Chairs
(one illustrated)
25 in. (63.5 cm.) wide; 41¾ in. (106 cm.) high; 29 in. (74 cm.) deep
London, 8 December 1994, £287,500 ($448,500)

This pair of 'walnut tree chairs stuffed & covd with green velvet gilt

frames' was supplied to Sir Robert Walpole, later 1st Earl of Orford (1676-1745) for the *Cabinett* or *Cov'd or Wrought Bedchamber* at Houghton. From a suite of twenty-two side chairs, an easy chair and two settees, they were almost certainly executed by the Roberts family of *The Royal Chair*, Marylebone Street, and are covered in the characteristic green silk-velvet upholstery, emblematic of Venus, which Kent employed to such great effect in the State Apartments at Houghton.

Attributed to RICHARD ROBERTS (British, d.1729), upholstery attributed to THOMAS PHILL (English, early 18th Century)
A George II gilt-gesso open Armchair
32½ in. (82.5 cm.) wide; 38½ in. (98 cm.) high; 30¼ in. (77 cm.) deep
London, 8 December 1994, £287,500 ($448,500)

This majestic throne (with bacchic lion's paws and Jupiter's eagle arms) can be identified with that supplied for the Coronation of Queen Caroline in 1727. Executed under the direction of William Kent by Richard Roberts (d.1729), carver and joiner to the Royal Household, it was upholstered by Thomas Phill, upholsterer to King George II. The chair is first recorded by Sir Matthew Decker on his visit to Houghton in 1728, when he remarked upon 'the costly chair wherein the present Queen was crowned', placed in the principal Blue Bedchamber.

Attributed to JAMES MOORE (British, 1670-1726)
A Pair of George I gilt-gesso open Armchairs (one illustrated)
29½ in. (75 cm.) wide; 47¾ in. (121.5 cm.) high;
29½ in. (75 cm.) deep
London, 8 December 1994, £881,500 ($1,375,140)

These armchairs were almost certainly commissioned by James Brydges, 1st Earl of Carnarvon and later 1st Duke of Chandos (1673-1744) for the 'Best Chamber' at Cannons, Middlesex. The suite is recorded in the inventory of 1725 as a 'Rich Crimson flower'd velvett (with a gold ground) bed, ... four elbow chairs, 8 back stools, 2 square do.' Executed under the direction of James Gibbs (1682-1754) by James Moore (1670-1726), cabinet-maker to King George I, the suite entered Houghton through its acquisition by George, 4th Earl and later 1st Marquess of Cholmondeley (1749-1827), for the Marble Parlour. The Cannons chairs achieved a world record auction price for a pair of armchairs.

ANDRÉ-CHARLES BOULLE (French, 1642-1732)
Two Louis XIV ebony and brass and pewter-inlaid brown
tortoiseshell *Coffres de Toilette* (*Mariage*)
(the *contre-partie* example illustrated)
27½ in. (70 cm.) wide; 48¾ in. (123 cm.) high; 20½ in. (52 cm.) deep
London, 8 December 1994, £1,541,500 ($2,404,740)

As early as 1684, André-Charles Boulle, *ébéniste, ciseleur et doreur du roi*,
delivered a *coffret* for the Grand Dauphin's *appartements* at the château de

Versailles. The enduring popularity of this design was confirmed by
the fire of 1720 in Boulle's Louvre ateliers in which 'douze coffres,
avec leurs pieds du differentes grandeurs et formes' were destroyed.
Usually supplied as single *coffres de toilette*, this matched pair in
*première* and *contre-partie* marquetry was almost certainly acquired by
Baron François-Alexandre Seillière (d. 1850) for the château de
Mello. Sold in Paris in 1911, they were purchased by Sir Philip
Sassoon, Bt., for the Large Drawing-Room at 25 Park Lane and are
recorded there in Sir John Lavery's picture, *The Red Hat* of 1925.

A Pair of gold-mounted
jasper (*cailloux d'egitto*) Ewers
early 18th Century
4½ in. (11.5 cm.) wide;
12½ in. (32 cm.) high; 6 in. (15.2 cm.) deep
London, 8 December 1994,
£1,266,500 ($1,975,740)

*Right:*
A Pair of Louis XVI gilt-bronze and
Chinese powder-blue glazed porcelain
Vases and Covers
the porcelain first half 18th Century
12 in. (30.5 cm.) wide; 16¼ in.
(41.5 cm.) high
London, 8 December 1994,
£507,500 ($791,700)

A Pair of Louis XV gilt-bronze Swans
10½ in. (27.5 cm.) wide; 12¾ in.
(32.5 cm.) high
London, 8 December 1994,
£408,500 ($637,260)

# FRENCH FURNITURE

GILLES JOUBERT (1689-1775)
A Louis XVI ormolu-mounted tulipwood, amaranth, palisander and parquetry Commode
42 in. (107 cm.) wide; 35¾ in. (91 cm.) high; 20¾ in. (52.5 cm.) deep
Monaco, 1 July 1995, Fr.6,172,500 (£797,481)

This agate-topped and ormolu-enriched tulipwood commode, with its laurel-festooned cassolette and mosaiced tablets of golden roses in ribbon-trellised rosewood, was commissioned for Louis XV's château de Compiègne. It was supplied in 1774 for the *cabinet intérieur* of the King's grandson, Charles-Philippe, comte d'Artois, who had married in the previous year; and with its pair was executed under the direction of Gilles Joubert, who had held the Royal appointment as *ébéniste ordinaire du garde-meuble* since 1758. This well-documented commode bears the Louis XVI inventory numbers for 1786 and 1788, and was described at the time as a commode '*à la régence*'.

*Right:*
ANDRÉ-CHARLES BOULLE (1642-1732)
A Régence ormolu-mounted Boulle brass-inlaid ebony and tortoiseshell *Bureau Plat*
71 in. (180.25 cm.) wide; 31½ in. (80 cm.) high;
37 in. (94 cm.) deep
Sold by the Trustees of Baroness Lucas and Dingwall's Trust
London, 15 June 1995, £793,500 ($1,269,600)

A Louis XIV ormolu-mounted Boulle brass-inlaid brown tortoiseshell and ebony Commode
52 in. (132 cm.) wide; 32½ in. (83 cm.) high;
27 in. (68.5 cm.) deep
London, 8 December 1994, £265,500 ($415,773)

*Left:*
NICOLAS-QUINIBERT FOLIOT (1706-1776)
A Pair of Louis XV white-painted *Fauteuils en Bergère à la Reine*
(one illustrated), each stamped 'N.Q.Foliot'
New York, 26 October 1994, $250,000 (£152,500)
Bought by the château de Versailles. The chairs are now on display
in the *Salon du Compagnie* at the Petit Trianon.

This pair of chairs was made in 1771 for the comtesse du Barry's
*Cabinet* at the château de Saint-Hubert. They were subsequently
used by the Princesse de Lamballe in her salon at the château de
Fontainebleau.

FRANÇOIS-HONORÉ-GEORGES JACOB (1739-1814) and
GEORGES-ALPHONSE JACOB-DESMALTER (1770-1841)
A Charles X ormolu and bronze *Guéridon*
stamped ' .IACOB' and 'A.J.A.', the marble stencilled to the reverse
'ERVDERIB/COPONIAE-OSTIIM/MDCCLXXXXII/
... INTARSARIO'
22 in. (56 cm.) diameter; 30¾ in. (78.5 cm.) high
London, 15 June 1995, £106,000 ($169,918)

*Left below:*
PIERRE-PHILIPPE THOMIRE (1751-1843)
An Empire ormolu and patinated bronze-mounted green granite
*Cheminée*
signed 'Thomire Paris' twice
44¾ in. (113.5 cm.) high; 73½ in. (187 cm.) wide; 19 in. (48.5 cm.) deep
New York, 23 May 1995, $266,500 (£169,745)

This *cheminée* was supplied circa 1809 to General Lemarois for his
*hôtel* on the rue de Grammont, Paris.

*Above:*
ADAM WEISWEILER (1744-1820)
A Louis XVI ormolu-mounted ebony and Japanese black and gold
lacquer *Commode à Vantaux*
stamped 'A. Weisweiler JME' twice
37 in. (94 cm.) high; 58 in. (148 cm.) wide; 21½ in. (54.5 cm.) deep
New York, 26 October 1994, $992,500 (£605,183)

GEORG HAUPT (1741-1784)
A Gustaf III ormolu-mounted amaranth, birch, marquetry and
parquetry *Secrétaire à Abattant*
37½ in. (95.5 cm.) wide; 48 in. (122 cm.) high;
107¾ in. (27.5 cm.) deep
London, 8 December 1994, £375,500 ($588,033)

This *secrétaire à abattant* was acquired from Österby Bruk by Baron
Gustaf Tamm before 1888 and remained in the family until it was
sold in 1963. It is closely related to a pair of *secrétaires* made by
Georg Haupt for Gustaf III in 1778, which remain at Tullgarn Slott.
Haupt, the most accomplished Swedish cabinet-maker, had
introduced the neo-classical style to Sweden in 1769 after his
return as *hovsnickare*, or *ébéniste du roi*, from his extensive travels to
Amsterdam, Paris and London.

GUSTAF ADOLPH DITZINGER (1760-1800)
A Gustaf III ormolu-mounted sycamore, tulipwood, amaranth
and marquetry Side Table
inscribed '1814/Förf: af G A Ditzinger 1791/23' in ink
34¾ in. (88 cm.) wide; 30 in. (76.5 cm.) high;
25½ in. (64.5 cm.) deep
London, 8 December 1994, £221,500 ($346,869)

This side table was recorded at Kronovall Castle, Sweden, then the
seat of Countess Alexandrine Anne Maria Hamilton and Count
Carl Gustaf Sparre of Sövdeborg, in the late nineteenth century.
It is probably the pair to a side table sold from Count Hamilton's
collection at Hedensberg in 1915. It appears to be the only table by
Gustaf Adolph Ditzinger to be signed and dated 1791. Ditzinger,
who was Georg Haupt's apprentice between 1776 and 1784 and
married Haupt's widow, had at this point already worked with
Louis Masreliez, Court Intendant, supplying furniture in the new
Italian style for Haga Pavilion, Gustaf III's country residence.

PIETRO PIFFETTI
(Italian, 1700-1777)
A rococo ivory, mother-of-pearl
and tortoiseshell-inlaid Coffer
circa 1748-51
8 in. (20.5 cm.) high;
10¼ in. (26 cm.) wide;
6¾ in. (17.5 cm.) deep
New York, 23 May 1995,
$299,500 (£190,764)

A Pair of German ormolu-mounted
tulipwood, amaranth and
marquetry serpentine Commodes
(one illustrated)
third quarter 18th Century
59½ in. (151 cm.) wide;
35½ in. (90 cm.) high;
28 in. (71 cm.) deep
London, 8 December 1994,
£232,500 ($364,095)

*Clockwise, from top left:*
A Russian ormolu *Guéridon*
early 19th Century
16¾ in. (42.5 cm.) diameter;
32 in. (81 cm.) high
Monaco, 1 July 1995,
Fr.1,300,500 (£167,959)

A Pair of Italian cream-painted and
parcel-gilt *Marquises* (one illustrated)
late 18th Century
Monaco, 1 July 1995,
Fr.908,500 (£117,377)

An Italian neo-classical giltwood Centre Table
circa 1800
47¾ in. (108.5cm.) high
New York, 26 October 1994,
$255,500 (£155,793)
This was supplied to Duca Luigi Braschi-
Onesti for the Palazzo Braschi, Rome.

# AMERICAN TASTE AND EUROPEAN FURNITURE

## by William J. Iselin

The geographic and social distance that separates the two continents has always determined America's approach to European works of art. Throughout the twentieth century, Americans have embraced and reinterpreted different aspects of European culture. Several collections came on the market at Christie's during the last season which marvellously represented American taste for acquiring and arranging European objects in a peculiarly American context.

Henry Francis du Pont's collection of European furniture and tapestries showed a side of a man who embodied the spirit of American decorative arts collecting in this country. He assembled the European furniture for his New York Park Avenue apartment with the same precision and fanatical eye for detail that manifested itself at Winterthur. In keeping with American taste of the twenties and thirties, du Pont arranged the principal reception rooms along national lines: an Italianate hall, French drawing room and English dining room and library. The superb set of eighteen dining-chairs made by Thomas Chippendale for Brocket Hall and acquired by du Pont for $10,000 from Partridge in 1923, formed the centrepiece of the dining room on Park Avenue. Ever the sensible man, du Pont replaced all the seat-rails to ensure that none of the chairs would collapse beneath his dinner guests! When the set returned to the market last October, they made $321,500.

Like virtually every important American collector of the time, du Pont turned to the New York firm of French & Co., for assistance not only with acquiring antiques but also with decorating. du Pont corresponded regularly and voluminously with Mitchell Samuels, the owner of French & Co., about the fabrics to be used on his seat furniture (he preferred eighteenth-century Italian silk brocades). He also bought a large Régence fauteuil covered in Beauvais tapestry which had been in the Hoentschel Collection from the firm in 1924 for $2,400 which reached $47,300 in the du Pont sale. Its combination of carved surfaces and rich fabric was characteristic of du Pont and indeed American preference of French furniture.

French & Co. also played an important role in the decoration of another quintessentially American house, Mar-A-Lago. Set in seventeen acres of Palm Beach Florida, Mar-A-Lago was built as a winter 'cottage' by Marjorie Merriweather Post and her husband, E.F. Hutton between 1923 and 1927 at a cost of $2.5million. Heavy in Spanish and Mediterranean influences in the architecture and furnishings, Mar-A-Lago typified the American passion for interiors on a baronial scale; the dining room had a ceiling inspired by a room in the Chigi Palace in Rome and could seat 45 around a table made specially for the room by French & Co. Mrs. Post also commissioned from the Società Civile Arte del Museo in Florence in 1927 a smaller pietra dura table for the room which sold for $48,300 when the contents of Mar-A-Lago were auctioned by Donald Trump on March 30 in New York.

This grand scale of collecting gave way to a more intimate approach to European decorative arts during the 1950s and 1960s. Alice Tully's New York apartment was a wonderful reflection of American fascination with classical eighteenth-century French furniture. High above Central Park, Miss Tully created an enfilade of reception rooms and intimate salons filled with Louis XV and Louis XVI pieces skillfully combined with Renaissance bronzes and Impressionist paintings. The Red Room, her principal drawing room, featured a *meuble d'appui* attributed to the ébéniste Guillaume Beneman (sold for $167,500) framed by a pair of early Louis XV *fauteuils à la reine* by Père Gourdin (sold for $96,000). While decidedly feminine in scale, Miss Tully's apartment provided a suitable setting for a rich and cultured woman. Indeed, each of these three collections in their own way illustrates a different aspect of the combination of American taste (and money) and European works of art.

The Dining Room of H. F. du Pont's private residence at Winterthur

*Above:*
The Red Room in Alice Tully's apartment

*Right:*
The Dining Room at Mar-A-Lago,
Palm Beach, Florida

Attributed to JAMES MOORE (1670-1726) and
JOHN GUMLEY (1691-1727)
The Holme Lacy Chandelier
A George I giltmetal-mounted gilt-gesso eight-light Chandelier
circa 1715
46 in. (117 cm.) high; 46 in. (117 cm.) diameter
New York, 22 April 1995, $717,500 (£448,438)

This splendid George I chandelier, with its eight acanthus-scrolled branches accompanied by masks of the moon-goddess Diana, is designed in the French 'arabesque' manner popularised around 1700 by King William III's architect Daniel Marot (1663-1752) through the publication of his goldsmith's pattern-book *Nouveau Livre d'Orfèvrerie.* It was one of a pair commissioned by James, 3rd Viscount Scudamore (1684-1716) and is likely to have been manufactured by James Moore and John Gumley, court cabinet-makers to King George I, for Holme Lacy, Herefordshire, where it was illustrated *in situ* in C. Latham's *In English Homes,* 1909.

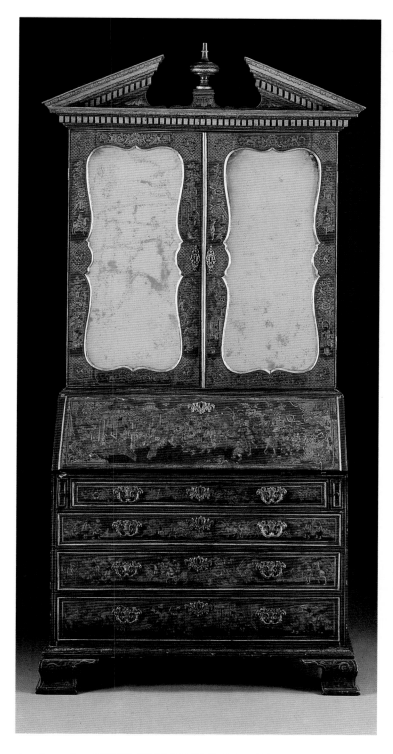

Attributed to GILES GRENDEY (1693-1780)
A George II scarlet and gilt-japanned Bureau-Cabinet
circa 1740
93 in. (236 cm.) high; 47 in. (120 cm.) wide; 26 in. (66 cm.) deep
New York, 22 April 1995, $233,500 (£145,938)

An early Georgian burr and figured walnut Tallboy
70½ in. (179 cm.) high; 39½ in. (100.5 cm.) wide; 21¾ in. (55 cm.) deep
London, 6 April 1995, £78,500 ($126,542)
Record auction price for an English tallboy

This cabinet is virtually identical to a cabinet bearing the trade label of Giles Grendey. The dense and exotic decoration compares closely to pieces from the well-known suite supplied by Grendey for the Duke of Infantado's castle at Lazcano, Spain. Many examples from this suite are now in public collections, including the Metropolitan Museum of Art, New York, and the Victoria and Albert Museum, London.

*Above:*
The Langley Park Tables
A Pair of George II mahogany Side Tables
(one illustrated)
35 in. (89 cm.) high; 60 in. (152.5 cm.) wide;
30 in. (76 cm.) deep
Sold from the collection of
Sir Christopher Proctor-Beauchamp, Bt.
London, 6 July 1995, £452,500 ($719,475)

These richly-carved mahogany pier-tables with *verde antico* slabs formed part of the furnishings commissioned in the mid-1740s by Sir William Beauchamp-Proctor, 1st Bt. (1722-1773), for the Palladian dining-room created by the Norwich architect Matthew Brettingham (1699-1769) at Langley Park, Norfolk.

*Left:*
A Pair of George II white-painted
Console Tables (one illustrated)
circa 1730
35 in. (89 cm.) high; 38 in. (97 cm.) wide;
23 in. (59 cm.) deep
New York, 20 January 1995, $189,500 (£119,182)

A Pair of George II mahogany library open Armchairs
(one illustrated)
Sold from the collection of the late Anthony Edgar, Esq.
London, 6 July 1995, £232,500 ($369,675)

This pair of richly-carved mahogany armchairs with their trellised
and acanthus-scrolled frames, are designed in the French

picturesque style popularised by Thomas Chippendale's *Gentleman
and Cabinet-Maker's Director* of 1754 and relate to a design in the
Metropolitan Museum of Art, New York. The chairs formed part
of a George II drawing-room suite that was almost certainly
commissioned by Dudley North (d. 1764) for Glemham Hall,
Suffolk. Their needlework, with birds in flower-festooned
vignettes, is likely to have been executed by Lady Barbara North
and corresponds to her watercolour pattern published in Percy
Macquoid's *History of English Furniture*, London, 1906, III, fig. 189.

The Craven Urns and Pedestals
A Pair of late George II mahogany dining-room Urns and
Pedestals
the pedestals 22½ in. (57 cm.) square,
72½ in. (184 cm.) high, overall
Sold from the collection of Jeremy Cotton, Esq., Tythrop Park
London, 27 April 1995, £496,500 ($800,854)

This magnificent pair of richly-carved George II mahogany
sideboard-pedestals with bacchic goat-headed and pelt-draped
urns and ormolu dolphin taps are likely to have been
commissioned by Fulwar, 4th Baron Craven (d. 1764). They may
have been executed for Craven's London mansion in Drury Lane
by Thomas Chippendale (1718-1779), cabinet-maker and
upholsterer of St. Martin's Lane, whose *Gentleman and Cabinet-
Maker's Director*, 1754-63, featured related patterns for banqueting
or dining-room furniture. They were later moved to Combe
Abbey, Warwickshire, where they were illustrated in H. Avray
Tipping's *English Homes*, 1929.

MATTHEW BOULTON (1728-1809)
A Pair of George III ormolu Perfume-Burners
15¼ in. (39 cm.) high; 5¼ in. (13.5 cm.) wide, overall
Sold from the collection of Viscount Villiers
London, 17 November 1994, £276,500 ($434,658)
Record auction price for a piece by Matthew Boulton

These ormolu cassolettes, formed as tripod 'sacred-urns' on bacchic altar-pedestals, were manufactured in 1771 by Messrs. Boulton and Fothergill of Birmingham and sold in April the following year for 28gns. at Matthew Boulton's sale at Christie's. The pair of 'Elegant Or Molee tripods' with siren *monopodiæ* were purchased by Robert Child (1739-1782) and were listed in the 1782 inventory of his drawing-room at Osterley Park House, Middlesex.

*Top:*
A George III giltwood Side Table, the design attributed to
Sir William Chambers (1723-1796)
35½ in. (90 cm.) high; 88 in. (224 cm.) wide; 30 in. (76 cm.) deep
London, 17 November 1994, £91,700 ($144,152)
Now at the Courtauld Institute of Art, Somerset House

This side table was commissioned in the late 1760s by Granville
Leveson-Gower, 2nd Earl Gower for Gower House, Whitehall.

*Above:*
Attributed to JOHN MAYHEW (1736-1811)
and WILLIAM INCE (1758/9-1804)
A George III sabicu, ebony and ebonised Commode, circa 1765
35 in. (89 cm.) high; 56 in. (142 cm.) wide; 28 in. (71 cm.) deep
New York, 15 October 1994, $244,500 (£154,747)

This commode was probably supplied to the 2nd Marquess of
Rockingham for Wentworth Woodhouse, Yorkshire. It relates to
other pieces from this house which share definite characteristics of
work by this firm and appears to be part of a large commission.

*Top:*
Attributed to JOHN MAYHEW (1736-1811) and
WILLIAM INCE (1758/9-1804)
A Pair of George III sabicu and marquetry Commodes
(one illustrated)
35¾ in. (91 cm.) high; 53 in. (134.5 cm.) wide; 26 in. (66 cm.) deep
Sold from the collection of Jeremy Cotton, Esq., Tythrop Park
London, 27 April 1995, £320,500 ($516,966)

*Above:*
THOMAS CHIPPENDALE (1718-1779)
A George III ormolu-mounted satinwood and
marquetry Commode
35½ in. (90 cm.) high; 57½ in. (146 cm.) wide;
24½ in. (65 cm.) deep
London, 6 July 1995, £331,500 ($527,085)

# AMERICAN FURNITURE

## *THE COLLECTION OF MR. AND MRS. EDDY NICHOLSON*

### *by John Hays*

During the 1980s, Eddy G. Nicholson emerged as one of the premier collectors of American furniture and decorative arts. His presence at auctions enlivened the market and infused it with a fresh spirit of competition that resulted in record prices for a Chippendale piecrust tea table, a William and Mary carved wainscot armchair, a Philadelphia silver tea service and a needlework hunt scene that was also made in Philadelphia.

Mr. Nicholson, a son of Texas, was inspired to collect by a deep and abiding love of American history. Over the years he became a serious student of the various carvers and artisans who had worked in colonial port cities including Newport, Boston, Portsmouth, New Hampshire, as well as Philadelphia and New York. Like many of the original owners of the furniture he collected, Mr. Nicholson pursued the finest examples possible, many of which he displayed in his nineteenth-century farmhouse in Hampton Falls, New Hampshire. In addition to their important examples of American furniture, Eddy Nicholson and his wife, Linda, also amassed one of the most complete collections of Dedham pottery. Together the Nicholsons supported the decorative arts in an academic way and helped fund publications like the recent survey of Portsmouth furniture, *Portsmouth Furniture* (Brock Jobe ed., New England, 1993).

When the Nicholsons decided to sell their collection, it was clear that this would arouse much interest: many prices paid during the peak of the American furniture market in the 1980s were surpassed. The Chippendale tea table, which had been the first piece of American furniture to fetch more than $1,000,000 at auction in 1986, sold for $2,400,000 – more than doubling its purchase price. As a whole, the collection realized $14,000,000 in a sale conducted over two days – an all time record for any single-owner sale of American decorative arts. The impact of the Nicholson sale's success was evident in the numerous headlines that proclaimed the return of the American furniture and decorative arts market. Overall, the auction of the Nicholson Collection can be regarded as a perfect demonstration that prime examples of furniture, silver and decorative arts that are fresh to the market can bring extraordinary results at auction.

*Above:*
The Willing-Francis-Fisher-Cadwalader family Chippendale carved mahogany Easy Chair
Philadelphia, circa 1770
45½ in. (115.6 cm.) high
New York, 28 January 1995, $618,500 (£389,655)

*Right:*
A Chippendale mahogany serpentine-front *bombé* Chest-of-Drawers
Shop of John Cogswell, Boston, 1775-85
31¼ in. (79.4 cm.) high; 36⅛ in. (91.8 cm.) wide; 20¼ in. (51.5 cm.) deep
New York, 28 January 1995, $574,500 (£361,935)

A Queen Anne carved mahogany Tea Table with slides
Boston, Massachusetts, 1740-60
26¾ in. (68 cm.) high; 30 in. (76.2 cm.) wide; 18¾ in. (47.6 cm.) deep
New York, 28 January 1995, $552,500 (£348,075)

A Chippendale carved mahogany Tea Table
Philadelphia, 1760-80
27½ in. (69.9 cm.) high; 32⅞ in. (83.5 cm.) diameter
New York, 28 January 1995, $2,422,500 (£1,526,175)

The arrival of highly skilled London trained carvers in Philadelphia during the mid-1760s such as Hercules Courtenay (1744?-1787) resulted in some of the most urbane and accomplished

manifestations of the eighteenth-century British Rococo in America.

Several features of the table illustrated here relate it to the work of Courtenay, as well as to a superlative piecrust tea table attributed to him in the collection of the Metropolitan Museum of Art. In addition to the multiple leaf overlays characteristic of Courtenay's work, a direct comparison of the two reveals the top of each shares the same distinctive wood grain, thus suggesting they were not only cut from the same flitch, but were products of the same shop.

*Above:*
A Tournai Falconry Tapestry
circa 1490
81½ x 99¼ in. (204 x 252 cm.)
London, 18 May 1995,
£210,500 ($330,485)

PIETRO FERLONI
(Italian, active 1717-1770)
A Roman San Michele a Ripa
Tapestry of the Creation of Eve,
after Raphael
159 x 140 in. (404 x 356 cm.)
London, 15 December 1994,
£95,000 ($148,200)

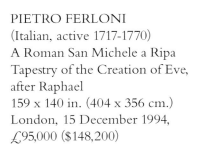

# SILVER

A Nautilus Cup and Cover, with silver-gilt mounts
probably North German, circa 1600, unmarked
10⅝ in. (27 cm.) high
Sold from the collection of M. and Mme. Robert Kahn Sriber
Monaco, 1 July 1995, Fr.953,300 (£123,165)

Attributed to JAN DE NAGHEL (Flemish, active c.1560-1570)
A Flemish parcel-gilt Cup in the form of an Owl
Ghent, circa 1560
7 in. (18 cm.) high, (355 ozs.)
Geneva, 15 May 1995, S.Fr.256,500 (£135,356)

*Right:*
ELIE PACOT (French, active c.1680-1713)
A Pair of silver Jardinières
Lille, 1709-10
4¾ in. (12 cm.) high; 11½ in. (29 cm.) wide, (4,500 grs.)
Geneva, 15 November 1994, S.Fr.399,500 (£195,833)

HENRI AUGUSTE (French, 1759-1816)
A Pair of Louis XVI silver Soup Tureens, Covers, Stands and Liners
Paris, 1787
21½ in. (54.5 cm.) length of stands, (663 ozs.)
New York, 11 April 1995, $772,500 (£482,813)

*Left:*

PIERRE HARACHE II (British, b.1653)
A William III silver-gilt Sideboard Dish
London, 1700
Britannia Standard
23½ in. (59.5 cm.) diameter, (172 ozs.)
Sold from the collection of the
Cholmondeley Family and the late
Sir Philip Sassoon, Bt., from
Houghton Hall, Norfolk
London, 8 December 1994,
£177,500 ($276,900)

JOHN HUGH LE SAGE
(British, c.1694–c.1750)
A George I silver-gilt Bowl and Cover
London, 1725
11¼ in. (28.5 cm.) wide; 9½ in. (24.2 cm.)
high; 8⅛ in. (20.5 cm.) deep, (76 ozs.)
Sold from the collection of the
Cholmondeley Family and the late
Sir Philip Sassoon, Bt., from
Houghton Hall, Norfolk. London,
8 December 1994, £111,500 ($173,940)

*Above:*

PHILIP ROLLOS II (British, 1678–c.1728)
A Pair of Queen Anne silver-gilt Cups,
Covers and matching Salvers, circa 1714
the cups and covers 14 in. (35.5 cm.) wide;
15¼ in. (38 cm.) high; 8 in. (20.5 cm.) deep
the salvers 15¾ in. (40.4 cm.) diameter;
5¼ in. (13.5 cm.) high, (483 ozs.)
Sold from the collection of the Cholmondeley
Family and the late Sir Philip Sassoon, Bt.,
from Houghton Hall, Norfolk. London,
8 December 1994, £800,000 ($1,248,000)

*Left:*
LOUIS METTAYER (British, active c.1700, d.1740)
The York Gold Cup, 1713
London, 1713
7 in. (17.8 cm.) high, (23 ozs.)
London, 12 July 1995, £205,000 ($325,950)

Attributed to PHILIP ROLLOS II (British, 1678-c.1728)
A Set of three Queen Anne silver-gilt Casters
circa 1705
10¼ in. (26 cm.) and 8 in. (20.5 cm.) high, (56 ozs.)
Sold by the Executors of the late Mrs. A.C. Vernon-Wentworth
London, 8 December 1994, £139,000 ($217,674)

*Above:*
A rococo silver, silver-gilt, 'Girl-in-a-Swing' porcelain and
polished steel-mounted dressing-table Casket surmounted by an
arched triple Looking Glass with folding doors
circa 1755, perhaps the St. James's factory of Charles Gouyn
the casket 10⅝ in. (27 cm.) wide
the mirror 13¾ in. (35 cm.) high
18 in. (45 cm.) high overall
London, 8 December 1994, £364,500 ($570,807)

TIFFANY & CO (American)
The 'Conglomerate' Vase, New York, 1878
20¼ in. (51.5 cm.) high, (91 ozs.)
Sold from the collection of Mr. and Mrs. Eddy Nicholson
New York, 27 January 1995, $211,500 (£133,019)

ODIOT (French)
A silver Table Service for twenty-four settings
Paris, 1920-21
Geneva, 15 May 1995, S.Fr.1,983,500 (£1,100,000)
Record auction price for twentieth-century silver

If the name of Odiot instantly conjures up memories of Napoleon's Imperial pomp, it should also be associated with the new and unprecedented popularity of French silver with the upper classes of nineteenth-century European society.

Maison Odiot had during the Empire already secured important commissions: the sceptre and the sword for the Emperor's coronation in 1804; large table services for Madame Mère (mother of the Emperor), Jérôme Bonaparte, King of Westphalia, and for Maximilian Joseph, King of Bavaria, all in 1806; a toilet set for the new Empress, Marie-Louise, and an extraordinary silver-gilt cot for the Emperor's son, both in 1810. Odiot's client list of the Empire period includes all the great Marshalls: Bernadotte, Berthier, Davout, Lannes, Masséna, Murat, Ney, Poniatowski; and also Talleyrand, Madame Récamier and many other high dignitaries and social figures. Napoleon's downfall did not stop Odiot's success. Even larger commissions were placed by the new rulers of the day. King Louis XVIII, Tsar Alexander I, Prince Metternich and the Duke of Wellington were frequent visitors to the Odiot establishment near the Palais Royal. Great table services were soon completed for two wealthy foreign clients: for Count Nikolai Demidoff in 1817, and for Count Branicki of Poland in 1819.

During the course of the nineteenth century, Odiot services came to decorate the most refined tables in Europe: aristocrats such as the duchesse d'Orléans and the duc de Luynes as well as 'nouveaux riches' (Salomon de Rothschild, Léopold Goldschmidt) purchased Odiot silver for it symbolised

the extravagant quality of their lifestyle.

Foreign clients came to Odiot too. This tradition, started by Count Branicki and Prince Demidoff, both immensely wealthy and eager to emulate French lifestyle, was perpetuated throughout the nineteenth century. The very last of these great commissions was placed with Maison Odiot in the aftermath of the First World War by Ali Bey Fahmy, a young, extremely wealthy and Europe-orientated Egyptian. The 'Prince of the Young' – as he was nicknamed in international circles – was to have a brief, but intense and extraordinarily refined life.

The service he commissioned from Maison Odiot in 1920 had more than a thousand pieces: complete with everything conceivable for 24 settings from the large candelabra, the majestic wine coolers, the impressive tureens, the extensive flatware, to toothpick-stands and menu-holders. It even featured 'assiettes à marrons chauds' (hot chestnut plates), a rare model adapted from Russian tableware. Designed mostly after famous Odiot models of the Empire period (still in Maison Odiot's possession), and made with exactly the same techniques, it was to join the numerous historic pieces of furniture, tapestries and *objets d'art* selected by the Prince from all over Europe.

The service was delivered by Maison Odiot in 1921, but the Prince hardly had the opportunity to use it; for he died in 1923. The service had never been used since. It was offered complete with its seventeen original cases, a touching testimony of the Egyptian Prince's dream of French culture and refinement.

# PORTRAIT MINIATURES

*Clockwise, from top left:*
CHRISTIAN FRIEDRICH ZINCKE
(German, 1683/4-1767)
A fine George II enamel and gold
Portrait Box, containing four enamels
open to show miniatures of Mrs. Delany
(1700-1788) and a lady in profile
ovals, 1¾ in. (4.4 cm.) high
London, 8 March 1995,
£43,300 ($70,579)

JOHN SMART (British, 1742-1811)
A Gentleman
signed with initials and dated 1774
silver-gilt frame surmounted with rose-
cut diamond ribbon cresting
oval, 1½ in. (3.8 cm.) high
London, 8 March 1995,
£10,350 ($16,870)

GEORGE ENGLEHEART
(British, 1750-1829)
Lady Burrell Blunt
signed with monogram
oval, 3 in. (7.5 cm.) high
London, 9 November 1994,
£27,600 ($44,436)

HEINRICH-FRIEDRICH FÜGER
(German, 1751-1818)
Three young Ladies
signed and dated 1791
4½ in. (11.7 cm.) diameter
Geneva, 15 November 1994,
S.Fr.113,500 (£55,637)

JOHANN-CHRISTIAN NEUBER
(German, 1736-1808)
A Saxon cameo-set gold and hardstone Snuff-Box
Dresden, circa 1770-80
3½ in. (8.7 cm.) wide
Sold from the collection of the late
Mrs. Vera Hue-Williams
Geneva, 16 May 1995, S.Fr. 181,700 (£98,118)

JEAN DUCROLLAY (French, 1709-after 1760)
A Louis XV gold and lacquer Snuff-Box
with the charge and discharge of Julien Berthe
Paris, 1753-4
3½ in. (8.7 cm.) wide
Geneva, 16 May 1995, S.Fr. 146,500 (£79,110)

The Orlov Box: a Russian gold-mounted porcelain
Snuff-Box
unmarked, the porcelain by the Imperial Porcelain Factory,
the mounts attributed to J. P. Ador
circa 1768
3½ in. (8.7 cm.) wide
London, 14 June 1995, £93,900 ($149,301)

# RUSSIAN WORKS OF ART

## THE WINTER EGG

### by Alexis de Tiesenhausen

The sale of the Winter Egg was, unquestionably, the main highlight of the Russian sale in Geneva on 16 November 1994, and the world record price of S.Fr.7,263,500 can be explained by the exceptional and unique background of this highly important Fabergé Imperial Easter Egg, given by Tsar Nicholas II to his mother, the Dowager Empress Maria Feodorovna, at Easter 1913.

The Tricentenary of the Romanov Dynasty was celebrated in 1913 with events throughout Russia, especially in St. Petersburg. Fabergé rose to the occasion and produced two eggs of arguably unsurpassed excellence. One was the Romanov Tricentenary Egg, presented to the Tsarina Alexandra Feodorovna, now in the State Museums of the Moscow Kremlin. The other was the Winter Egg.

The Winter Egg is one of the most creative and original of the Easter eggs Fabergé made for the Tsars. It symbolises the transition from Winter to Spring, the seed emerging to new life, the Resurrection. The Spring flowers appear as in a frosty mist through the Winter ice of the egg, before the egg is opened to reveal the surprise in its full detail. Only in the first Imperial Egg, the Hen Egg of 1885, and in the Resurrection Egg, probably made in 1887 (now both in the Forbes Magazine Collection) is the Easter message so clearly illustrated, but neither of these has the degree of realism and delicacy achieved in the Winter Egg.

Many of Fabergé's imperial eggs rely on standard Rococo and Neo-classical motifs, albeit superbly executed in gold and enamel, for their effect, but with the Winter Egg, Alma Theresia Pihl, its designer, broke away from the conventional elements to produce a magical work of original creative genius.

The egg sits on a rock crystal base which is formed as a block of melting ice, applied with platinum-mounted rose-diamond rivulets. The Egg itself is also of rock crystal, and is detachable, held vertically by a pin. It has rose-diamond set platinum borders graduating around the hinge and encompassing in the top a cabochon moonstone, painted in reverse with the date 1913.

The thinly carved and translucent shell of the egg is finely engraved on the interior to simulate ice crystals and the outside is further engraved and applied with a similar rose-diamond and platinum design, opening vertically to reveal the full splendour of the surprise. The surprise is a platinum double-handled trelliswork basket, set with rose-diamonds and full of wood anemones, suspended from a platinum hook in the top of the egg. Each of these delicate flowers is realistically carved from a single piece of white quartz and has a gold wire stem and stamens. The centre of each open flower is set with a demantoid garnet, some are carved half open, some in bud and the pale green translucent leaves are delicately carved in nephrite, emerging from a bed of gold moss. The base of this exquisite basket of flowers is engraved 'FABERGÉ 1913'.

The Winter Egg was made in the workshop of Albert Holmström, which mainly specialised in jewellery. In 1903 he succeeded his father, August Holmstöm who had been appointed in 1857 as principal jeweller to Fabergé.

With the inspiration of the talented designer, Alma Theresia Pihl, whose two *pièces de résistance* were the Moscaic Egg, presented in 1914 (and now in the collection of Her Majesty the Queen), and the Winter Egg, presented in 1913, and under the direction of Albert Holmström, some of Fabergé's most outstanding works were created, of which the Winter Egg is indubitably one.

The Winter Egg is one of the best documented of all imperial Easter eggs, having been sold by the Soviet Government in the late 1920s, and the original invoice is still held in the Russian State Archives. It appeared first in a largely autobiographical book *Twice Seven* (London, 1933) written by Henry Charles Bainbridge, who had been manager of Fabergé's London branch. Since its last appearance on the market in 1949, the Winter Egg had never been exhibited and detailed colour photographs of the egg and its original surprise had never been published before its appearance in Christie's catalogue. It can therefore be considered as the last fully documented imperial egg ever to come on the market from a private source, as almost all of the known and documented imperial eggs are now in museums or well established collections.

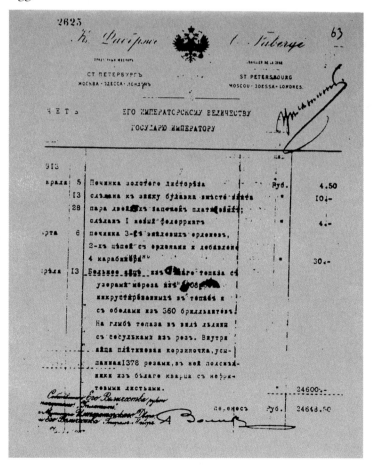

A copy of the original Fabergé invoice from the Russian State archives, kindly made available by V. V. Skurlov and Mrs. T. Fabergé due to the help of Alexander von Solodkoff of Ermitage, London

FABERGÉ
workmaster Albert Holmström (1876-1925)
The Winter Egg
An Imperial Easter Egg with original surprise
engraved 'FABERGÉ 1913'
overall height 5⅝ in. (14.2 cm.)
Geneva, 16 November 1994, SFr.7,263,500 (£3,560,539)

# JEWELLERY

## BLUE DIAMONDS

### by Simon Teakle

The awe and mystery of precious gems is indelibly linked with many cultures. The Shah Jahan, the Nizam of Hyderbad, King Louis XIV, Queen Victoria and the Sultan of Brunei are a few legendary names historically linked with the world's most precious gems. The amazing hypnotic hold that these stones have, continue to bewitch, and, in an era of satellite communication, silicon chips and supersonic travel, it is a sobering thought that these relatively small objects still retain absolute power. The enigma and romance of gems is classically illustrated in the world of coloured diamonds. They can manifest themselves throughout the spectrum – white and black, purple and orange, red and green, yellow and grey, pink and blue.

These are the ultimate prize for the collector: the allure is complex with a combination of obtaining something so small in relation to its immense value, knowing that these are the rarest of rare and of course experiencing the incredible beauty these stones radiate.

The colour of these stones can be remarkably complex with secondary and sometimes tertiary tones creeping in; orangy-pink, yellowish-green and greyish-blue – all are combinations regularly seen. However, it is when the pure pinks, greens and blues are found that the prized gems are recognised.

Jean-Baptiste Tavernier, the seventeenth-century gem merchant brought many of the great historic diamonds to France, where Louis XIV was an enthusiastic and able client. It is from this point that the recorded history of the few truly blue diamonds really begins.

Centuries ago, the blue diamonds of India came from the Kollur Mine in Golconda, and it was from this source that the first blue stones found their way to the Royal Courts of Europe. Almost all of the blue diamonds found today come from the Premier Mine in South Africa.

Of all the natural colours in which diamonds can be found, blue is one of the rarest and most desirable. Natural blue diamonds derive their beautiful hues from minute impurity atoms of boron, incorporated within the crystal lattice of the diamond during its crystallisation. They are members of the rare Type 11b category and are semi-conductors of electricity.

The majestic blue that is represented in the stone we sold in New York in April may be associated with the definition of blue in the English dictionary: 'a colour whose hue is that of the clear sky'. The beauty of this magnificent gem is that in any light, weak or strong, natural or artificial, depth of blue is apparent in a way that is breathtaking. A stone of this size and colour is a rare phenomenum: that it is also internally flawless is yet more remarkable. In the classic rule of the four c's (colour, clarity, carat and cut) every category is a paragon of excellence. A stone's rarity and value is dependant on the strength of colour as well as the clarity, cut and size.

For many years the Gemological Institute of America has laid out a consistent scale of grading for coloured diamonds but with an increasingly sophisticated audience the GIA have responded with an upgraded scale by which these stones are judged. Before, the colour of two blue diamonds for example, could have had the same grading but the value could differ by as much as 400%. One stone would have a waspish colour to it whilst the other could appear like the midnight sky. By describing more accurately the saturation colour this huge range can be dramatically reduced. In the case of blue diamonds instead of 'fancy blue' being the top accolade, there are now four other groups to describe the depth of colour. These grades are fancy vivid blue, fancy deep blue, fancy intense blue and fancy blue. One is not necessarily intended to be better than the other as they are describing tonality, however, fancy vivid and fancy deep have immediately taken precedence over anything else. The magnificent 13.49 carat flawless fancy deep blue diamond we sold was the first stone to receive this new top categorisation and was a perfect illustration of how a new grading set this regal gem apart. It was a diamond worthy of any collection in the world. Its beauty was breathtaking and $7,482,500 was an astonishing figure for an astonishing stone. Any buyer of gems will calculate his value on a per carat basis, whether he is buying small stones known as mêlée for as little of $100 per carat or an important single gem. The value he arrives at whether it is for a diamond, ruby, sapphire or emerald all revolves around this calculation. The price per carat for this blue diamond which calculated out at $554,700 is a world record price per carat for any blue diamond sold at auction.

On 28 April, 1987, Christie's sold also in New York a 0.95 carat red diamond for an unbelievable $880,000. The magnitude of this amount was considered to be a record that would stand for decades. However, the strength and confidence in the coloured diamond market over the past two years has climbed consistently and shows that nothing is forever and this blue diamond is suggesting to its smaller cousin that more spectacular results may not be far away.

Enlarged

*Right:*
A rectangular cut fancy deep blue
diamond Ring
13.49 carats
New York, 13 April 1995,
$7,482,500 (£4,714,000)

*Far right:*
An unmounted rectangular-cut fancy
blue Diamond
19.20 carats
Geneva, 17 November 1994,
S.Fr.8,143,500 (£3,990,300)

An unmounted rectangular-cut light
grey-blue Diamond
17.55 carats
Geneva, 17 November 1994,
S.Fr.1,103,800 (£702,400)

A marquise-cut fancy blue diamond Ring
5.38 carats
New York, 19 October 1994,
$1,982,500 (£1,229,150)

An unmounted rectangular-cut fancy
pink Diamond
19.66 carats
Geneva, 17 November 1994,
S.Fr.9,573,500 (£4,691,000)

A rectanglar-cut fancy orange pink
diamond Ring
18.65 carats
Geneva, 18 May 1995,
S.Fr.2,533,500 (£1,342,750)

A rectangular-cut fancy intense yellow
diamond Ring
7.20 carats
New York, 13 April 1995,
$607,500 (£382,725)

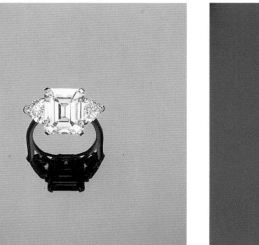 

An unmounted rectangular-cut fancy intense
yellow Diamond
26.92 carats
Geneva, 18 May 1995,
S.Fr.839,500 (£444,930)

*Top from left:*
A Burmese sapphire and diamond cluster Pendant
the sapphire 91.37 carats
Geneva, 17 November 1994, S.Fr.597,500 (£292,780)

BULGARI
A ruby and diamond two stone Ring
Geneva, 18 May 1995, S.Fr.608,500 (£322,500)

CARTIER
A Pair of sapphire and diamond Clips
circa 1935
New York, 13 April 1995, $40,250 (£25,360)

*Centre:*
An Art Deco ruby and diamond Bracelet
circa 1930
London, 21 June 1995, £65,300 ($104,500)

*Bottom, from left:*
VAN CLEEF & ARPELS
An invisibly-set ruby and diamond flower Brooch
New York, 13 April 1995, $173,000 (£109,000)

VAN CLEEF & ARPELS
An invisibly-set ruby and diamond twin leaf Brooch
circa 1960
London, 21 June 1995, £23,000 ($36,800)

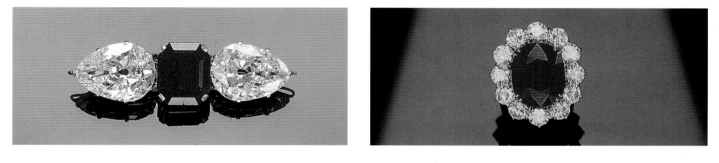

*Top:*
CARTIER
A ruby and diamond Necklace
circa 1935
Geneva, 19 May 1995, S.Fr.289,500
(£153,430)

*Centre, from left:*
A Burmese ruby and diamond Brooch
the ruby 18.18 carats
Geneva, 18 May 1995, S.Fr.850,500
(£450,760)

A Burmese ruby and diamond Ring
the ruby 21.04 carats
Geneva, 18 May 1995,
S.Fr.817,500 (£443,880)

*Above:*
VAN CLEEF & ARPELS
A ruby and diamond Bracelet
circa 1960
London, 21 June 1995, £42,200 ($67,500)

*Above, from left:*
JAR
A Pair of diamond bow Earclips
circa 1984
St. Moritz, 16 February 1995,
S.Fr.113,500 (£57,614)

A fancy pink and fancy yellowish green
diamond Brooch
New York, 13 April 1995,
$706,500 (£445,100)

An American marquise-cut diamond Ring
8.26 carats, E colour and VS1
New York, 19 October 1994,
$145,500 (£90,210)

The diamond is known as 'The Star of
Arkansas' and was discovered in 1956 at the
Crater of Diamonds State Park, 2½ miles
south of Murfreesboro, Arkansas.

*Left:*
A diamond pendant Necklace
New York, 13 April 1995,
$1,762,500 (£1,101,563)

*Right:*
An unmounted rectangular-cut Diamond
69.79 carats, D colour and flawless
New York, 13 April 1995,
$5,612,500 (£3,535,900)

*Far right:*
A rectangular-cut diamond Ring
30.75 carats, D colour and flawless
New York, 19 October 1994,
$2,422,500 (£1,502,000)

A marquise-cut diamond Ring
21.50 carats, D colour and VVS1
New York, 13 April 1995,
$662,500 (£417,380)

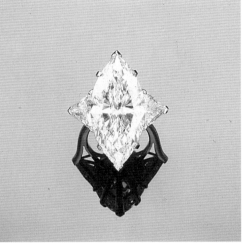

A pear-shaped diamond Ring
23.25 carats, F colour and flawless
New York, 19 October 1994,
$783,500 (£485,770)

An unmounted rectangular-cut Diamond
50.01 carats, D colour, loupe clean
Geneva, 17 November 1994,
S.Fr.3,305,500 (£1,618,720)

A rectangular-cut diamond Ring
16.56 carats, F colour and VS2
New York, 19 October 1994,
$376,500 (£233,430)

BULGARI
A rectangular-cut diamond Ring
25.15 carats
Geneva, 18 May 1995,
S.Fr.751,500 (£398,300)

BOUCHERON
A cushion-shaped diamond Ring
12.41 carats, D colour and VS2
London, 21 June 1995,
£309,000 ($495,200)

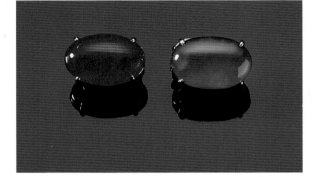

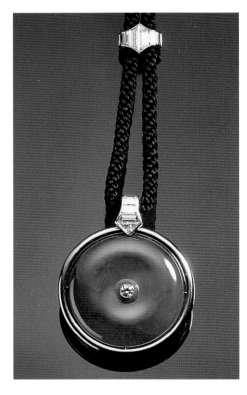

*Top left:*
CARVIN FRENCH
A coral, jadeite and coloured diamond Brooch
Hong Kong, 1 May 1995,
H.K.$2,880,000 (£231,074)

*Top right:*
BULGARI
A jadeite and gemset Pendant
Hong Kong, 1 May 1995,
H.K.$1,285,000 (£103,100)

*Clockwise, from bottom left:*
A Pair of 'Abacus Seed' Rings
Hong Kong, 1 May 1995, H.K.$3,540,000 (£284,000)

A Pair of jadeite and ruby Earclips
Hong Kong, 31 October 1994, H.K.$2,330,000 (£186,050)

BULGARI
A jadeite and diamond *Huaigu* Necklace
Hong Kong, 31 October 1994, H.K.$4,970,000 (£396,900)
A world record price for a 'Huaigu' sold at auction

A jadeite bar Brooch
Hong Kong, 1 May 1995, H.K.$3,540,000 (£284,000)

*Above:*
A jadeite bead Necklace
circa 1933
Formerly in the collection of Barbara Hutton and
Princess Nina Mdivani
Hong Kong, 31 October 1994,
H.K.$33,020,000 (£2,636,850)
Record auction price for Jadeite jewellery and the
most expensive item ever sold at auction in Asia

*Right:*
A jadeite Bangle
Hong Kong, 1 May 1995,
H.K.$12,120,000 (£972,439)
Record auction price for a jadeite Bangle

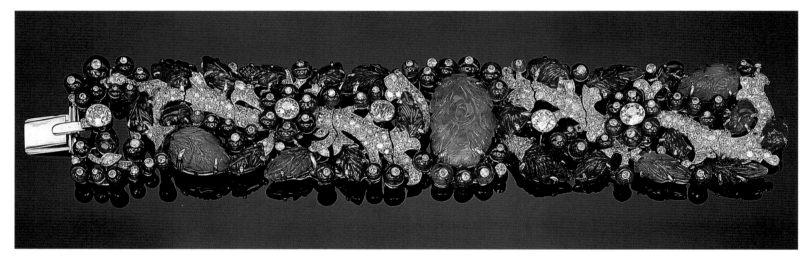

*Top:*
CARTIER
An Art Deco emerald and diamond
Bracelet
circa 1920
New York, 19 October 1994,
$85,000 (£52,700)

*Centre, from left:*
An emerald and diamond Brooch
the emerald 18.86 carats
New York, 19 October 1994,
$464,500 (£288,000)

A Pair of emerald and diamond
Brooches
Geneva, 18 May 1995,
S.Fr.531,500 (£281,700)

BULGARI
An emerald Ring
13.60 carats
Geneva, 18 May 1995,
S.Fr.487,500 (£258,380)

*Above:*
CARTIER
An emerald, ruby, sapphire and diamond
'Tutti Frutti' Bracelet
circa 1930
Geneva, 18 May 1995,
S.Fr.652,500 (£345,800)

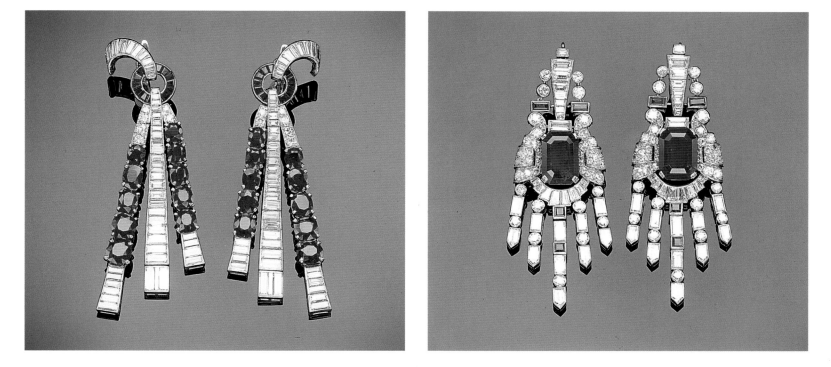

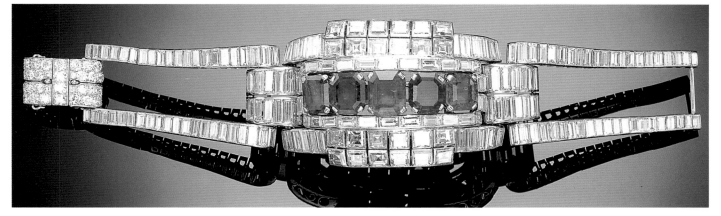

*Top, from left:*
A Pair of Art Deco ruby and diamond
Ear-Pendants
circa 1935
Geneva, 18 May 1995, S.Fr.104,700 (£55,490)

A Pair of Art Deco sapphire and
diamond Ear-Pendants
circa 1925
Geneva, 18 May 1995, S.Fr.212,500 (£112,600)

*Centre:*
An Art Deco emerald and diamond Bracelet
circa 1935
Geneva, 18 May 1995, S.Fr.179,500 (£95,135)

*Bottom, from left:*
A pear-shaped diamond Pendant
33.47 carats
Geneva, 18 May 1995,
S.Fr.575,500 (£305,000)

An antique pearl drop and diamond Pendant
Geneva, 18 May 1995,
S.Fr.267,500 (£141,775)

A rectangular-cut diamond Ring
23.79 carats, D colour VS1
Geneva, 18 May 1995,
S.Fr.1,048,500 (£555,700)

All from the collection of the late Mrs Vera Hue-Williams, sold in Geneva, 18 May 1995 for a total of S.Fr.7,311,695 (£3,909,470)

*Above, from left:*
A Pair of Victorian Brooches
circa 1850
London, 21 June 1995,
£51,000 ($81,600)

BOUCHERON
An antique sapphire and diamond Brooch
circa 1880
Geneva, 17 November 1994,
S.Fr.256,500 (£125,700)

*Left:*
CARTIER
A Belle Epoque diamond stomacher Brooch
circa 1910
Geneva, 17 November 1994,
S.Fr.289,500 (£141,850)

*Top:*
An antique pearl and diamond Necklace
circa 1820, London, 8 February 1995, £115,000 ($180,000)

This was formerly in the collection of Queen Josephine-
Maximilienne-Eugénie Napoléone (1807-1876), portrait inset,
who married King Oscar I, King of Sweden and Norway, in
Stockholm, 19 June 1823.

*Above:*
An antique emerald and diamond Bandeau
circa 1870
New York, 19 October 1994, $222,500 (£138,000)

# CERAMICS

*Left:*
An Urbino *Istoriato* tri-lobed shallow Basin from the Guidobaldo II Service, painted with scenes from the life of Joseph in the workshop of Orazio Fontana
circa 1575
18½ in. (47 cm.) wide
London, 12 June 1995, £78,500 ($125,207)

A Faenza Tondo, attributed to the Painter of the Caricatures
circa 1515
11 in. (28 cm.) diameter
New York, 10 January 1995, $107,000 (£68,590)

*Right, from top left:*
A Pair of Meissen chinoiserie two-handled Beakers and Saucers (one illustrated), painted by Johann Gregor Höroldt
blue crossed swords mark, circa 1725
London, 5 December 1994, £62,000 ($96,596)

A Meissen dated Figure of Hofnarr Fröhlich, modelled by Johann Joachim Kändler
blue crossed swords mark, 1739
9⅝ in. (24.5 cm.) high
Sold from the collection of the late
Sir Henry Tate, Bt.
London, 6 March 1995, £20,700 ($33,948)

A Meissen chinoiserie oval Sugar-Box and Cover
the mount with 'EA' for Elias Adam and Augsburg town mark for 1722-26
circa 1723
4¾ in. (12 cm.) wide
Sold from the collection of Dr. Sali Guggenheim
Geneva, 15 May 1995, S.Fr.69,000 (£36,898)

*Above, from left:*

A Vincennes *bleu celeste* pierced lozenge-shaped Basket from the Louis XV Service (*corbeille lozange*), blue interlaced L mark enclosing date letter C for 1755, painter's mark of Thévenet, 12¼ in. (31 cm.) wide
Sold by the Abercorn Heirlooms Trustees
London, 12 June 1995, £19,550 ($31,182)

A Vincennes *bleu celeste* pierced lozenge-shaped Basket from the Louis XV Service (*corbeille lozange*), blue interlaced L mark enclosing date letter B for 1754
12¼ in. (31 cm.) wide
Sold by the Abercorn Heirlooms Trustees
London, 12 June 1995, £20,700 ($33,016)

A Vincennes *bleu celeste* pierced lozenge-shaped Basket from the Louis XV Service (*corbeille lozange*), blue interlaced L mark enclosing date letter B for 1754 with a dot above and below, 12 in. (30.5 cm.) wide
Sold by the Abercorn Heirlooms Trustees
London, 12 June 1995, £21,850 ($34,850)

*Left, from top left:*
A Buen Retiro Italian comedy
Group of Spaghetti-eaters modelled
by Giuseppe Gricci
four blue *fleur-de-lys* marks, circa 1760
7¼ in. (18.5 cm.) high
London, 12 June 1995,
£40,000 ($63,800)

A Berlin gold-ground slender
Campana Vase and Plinth of
Wellington Service type
blue sceptre mark, *Pressnummer* '38',
painter's marks of a puce circle and
a yellow line, circa 1817
27¾ in. (70.5cm.) high overall
London, 5 December 1994,
£115,500 ($173,717)

A Frankenthal *Bataillenmalerei* Coffee
and Tea-Service of twenty-five
pieces, painted with martial scenes
by Winterstein (active 1758-1781)
crowned *Carl Theodor* mark and 'AB',
signed 'W' to one of the scenes,
1762-70
Amsterdam, 23 November 1994,
Fl.195,500 (£71,612)

*Right:*
A London (Southwark) Delft dated
blue and white Mug
1653
7½ in. (19 cm.) high
Sold by the Mount Stuart Trust
London, 5 December 1994,
£33,350 ($51,959)

An English creamware Botanical
part Dinner-Service of one hundred
and six pieces, each painted with a
named specimen flower
circa 1805
London, 5 December 1994,
£36,700 ($57,178)

*Above:*
A Pair of Jardinières by Pieter Adriaanson Koeks (one illustrated)
iron-red monogram of PAK for Pieter Adriaanson Koeks,
1705-10
19¼ in. (49 cm.) high
Sold from the collection of M. and Mme. Robert Kahn Sriber
Monaco, 1 July 1995, Fr.3,260,500 (£421,253)
Record auction price for European pottery

*Right:*
A pair of Dutch Delft polychrome dog Buttertubs and Covers
mid-18th Century
6½ in. (15.5 cm.) high
Amsterdam, 7 June 1995, Fl.41,400 (£16,494)

JONAS ZEUNER (1727-1814)
A Verre Églomisé of the Herengracht, Amsterdam and the Nieuwe
Herengracht, the Blauwbrug to the left, the Leprozengracht and
Houtgracht beyond
signed and dated 'Zeuner inv.ao 1776'
26⅝ x 36⅜ in. (68 x 92.5 cm.)
Amsterdam, 20 December 1994, Fl.195,500 (£71,091)
Record auction price for verre églomisé

# MODERN DECORATIVE ARTS

*Above:*
EMILE GALLÉ (French, 1846-1904)
A blue 'Rhododendron' mould-blown
overlaid and etched glass table Lamp
signed 'Gallé'
18¾ in. (47.6 cm.) high, 14¼ in. (36.2 cm.)
diameter of shade
New York, 1 April 1995, $222,500 (£137,950)

*Right:*
RENÉ LALIQUE (French, 1860-1945)
'Renard', a clear and frosted glass Mascot,
moulded as a Fox, acid-etched 'R. Lalique'
8¼ in. (21.5 cm.) length
New York, 10 December 1994,
$118,000 (£75,520)
Record auction price for a Lalique car mascot

EMILE GALLÉ (French, 1846-1904)
'L'Eternal Debat', a wheel-carved tristesse
glass Vase
engraved 'Emile Gallé Nancy fecit'
circa 1890
5¾ in. (14.4 cm.) high
New York, 10 December 1994, $134,500 (£86,080)

THOMAS MOLESWORTH (American, 1890-1977)
A wrought-iron and painted mica twelve-light
Chandelier
circa 1935-37
63 in. (160 cm.) high, 30 in. (76.2 cm.) diameter
Sold from the collection of furnishings from
Thomas Molesworth's 'Old Lodge'
New York, 7 June 1995, $57,500 (£36,164)

Designed by EDWARD WILLIAM GODWIN
(British, 1833-1886)
A carved oak 'Eagle' Chair
circa 1869-77
London, 5 May 1995, £18,400 ($29,660)

*Right, clockwise from top:*
JACQUES-EMILE RUHLMANN
(French, 1879-1933))
'Lit Soleil', an *ébène de macassar* Bed
branded 'Ruhlmann'
76½ in. (194.4 cm.) high; 71 in. (180.3 cm.) wide;
89½ in. (227.4 cm.) long,
New York, 10 December 1994, $167,500 (£107,200)

DR CHRISTOPHER DRESSER
(British, 1834-1904)
An Art Furnishers' Alliance gilt and ebonised wood
Side Chair
circa 1880
London, 16 November 1994, £20,700 ($32,706)

PIERRE CHAREAU (French, 1883-1950)
A walnut Table Eventail
circa 1923/4
32¼ in. (82 cm.) high
London, 5 May 1995, £44,400 ($71,572)

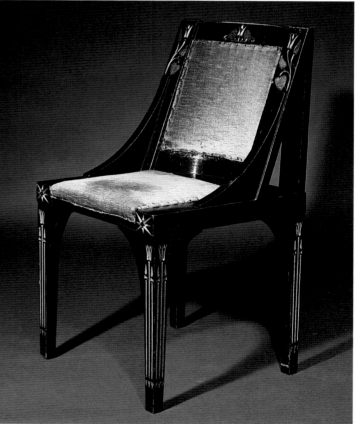

# THE HOLY GRAIL TAPESTRIES, DESIGNED BY SIR EDWARD COLEY BURNE-JONES FOR MORRIS & CO.

## by Nicola Redway

'The noblest of the weaving arts is tapestry ... It may be looked upon as a mosaic of pieces of colour made up of dyed threads, and is capable of producing wall ornament of any degree of elaboration within the proper limits of duly considered decorative work. As in all wall decoration, the first thing to be considered in the designing of tapestry is the force, purity and elegance of the silhouette of the object represented ... Depth of tone, richness of colour and exquisite gradations of tints are easily to be obtained in tapestry; and it also demands that crispness of and abundance of beautiful detail which was the especial characteristic of fully developed Medieval Art.'

So wrote William Morris in a lecture of 1888, less than ten years after he had taught himself the art and woven his first tapestry on a loom built in his bedroom at Kelmscott House. In 1881, the firm of Morris & Co. moved to larger premises at Merton Abbey in South London, and here Morris was finally able to fulfil his ambition of reviving the tapestry weaving industry in England. Three large looms were installed, and under the expert tutelage of J.H.Dearle, Morris's first apprentice who was later to become his chief weaver, assistant and designer, young boys were rapidly trained to become skilled practitioners in the 'noble art'.

Although Morris himself designed some of the earliest tapestries, the most successful works produced at Merton Abbey were certainly those designed by his close friend Sir Edward Burne-Jones, none more so than the set of six tapestries illustrating

the Quest of the Holy Grail. This magnificent narrative series of six tapestries was commissioned from Morris and Co. by the Australian mining millionaire William Knox D'Arcy for the dining room at his home, Stanmore Hall in Middlesex. These represent one of the finest artistic achievements of the Arts and Crafts movement. They also reflected Morris and Burne-Jones' devotion to Sir Thomas Malory's *Morte D'Arthur*, a work which the two friends first encountered in 1855 while still undergraduates at Oxford. In his later life, Burne-Jones was to return to this early source of inspiration in a number of his works, but it was the legend of the Quest of the Holy Grail which had the most profound effect on his imagination. 'Lord!', he wrote 'How that San Graal story is ever in my mind and thoughts continually. Was ever anything in the world beautiful as that is beautiful? If I might clear away all the work that I have begun, if I might live to clear it all away and dedicate the last days to that tale – if only I might.'

The physical features of the large and imposing dining room at Stanmore Hall were central factors in determining both the subject matter and scale of the narrative panels, which were to form a continuous frieze around the upper walls. Morris later recorded that the Quest was chosen for two reasons – firstly because he (and Burne-Jones) believed it to be the most beautiful and complete of the Arthurian legends, and secondly because the tale was 'in itself a series of pictures' and as such the most suitable subject for the

appointed setting. Burne-Jones' acknowledgement of the relation between the subject and the setting is clear from the towering scale of his figures, their heads in some cases deliberately cut to enhance the dramatic effect when viewed some thirteen feet from the ground. A number of scenes were considered by Morris and Burne-Jones before deciding on the final sequence of six, which showed *The Knights of the Round Table Summoned to the Quest by a Strange Damsel, The Arming and Departure of the Knights, The Failure of Sir Lancelot to enter the Chapel of the Holy Grail, The Failure of Sir Gawain, The Ship* (a small panel symbolising the transfer of the Quest to foreign lands) and finally *The Attainment of the Holy Grail by Sir Galahad, Sir Bors and Sir Percival.*

Although Burne Jones designed the figure studies for each panel, the exquisite *mille-fleurs* foregrounds and the decoration on the clothing were all designed by J. Henry Dearle, contributing much to the overall spirit of medievalism in the final design. The process by which these two artistic schemes were combined was unique to the Morris & Co. works; the original designs by Burne-Jones (no more than twenty inches high) were first photographed, with enlargements then being worked on and embellished by both Burne-Jones and Dearle, before finally being presented to the weavers for transfer to the loom. Although strictly following the overall design from the working cartoon, the young weavers were allowed considerable latitude in the interpretation of the subtlety of tint and shading, a consideration which Morris fully supported, maintaining that 'the executants themselves... [are] both in nature and training, artists, not merely animated machines.'

The immediate and extraordinary acclaim with which the Holy Grail tapestries at Stanmore Hall were received, marked a turning point in the fortunes of the Merton Abbey works, which were facing the very real threat of closure through lack of work. Employing the same principal weavers as for the original set, a further two weavings were commissioned from Morris & Co. The first, in 1895-6, was for a partial set of three panels with one verdure for Lawrence Hodson for the drawing room at Compton Hall. The second commission was for the only other complete set to be woven, received from D'Arcy's friend and business partner, George McCulloch, in 1898-9. After changing hands several times following McCulloch's death in 1913, the complete set was last sold at Christie's in 1953, for 350 guineas. *The Summons* from this group later re-appeared at auction in 1980, when it was acquired by Birmingham Museum and Art Gallery, and the small *Ship* has since been lost, but the remaining four tapestries were all offered in London in May, 1995, and sold for a total of £842,000 ($1,330,360).

*The Attainment* was the largest of the set, and indeed was the largest woven at Merton Abbey until 1935. It is also without doubt the most mystical and compelling of the Holy Grail series. Burne-Jones himself described its composition thus: 'We have passed out of Britain and are in the land of Sarras, the land of the soul, that is. And of all the hundred and fifty that went on the Quest, three only are chosen, and may set foot on that shore, Bors, Percival, and Galahad. Of these Bors and Percival may see the Grail afar off – three big angels bar their way and one holds the spear that bleeds; that is the spear that entered Christ's side, and it bleeds always. You know by its appearing that the Grail is near. And then comes Galahad who alone may see it – and to see it is death, for it is seeing the face of God.'

SIR EDWARD COLEY BURNE-JONES, Bt., A.R.A.
(English, 1833-1898)
'The Attainment of the Holy Grail by Sir Galahad, Sir Bors and Sir Percival', a Morris & Co. Merton Abbey Tapestry from the 'Quest of the Holy Grail' Series
94 in. (236 cm.) high, 236 in. (682 cm.) total width
London, £331,500 ($523,770)

# ANTIQUITIES

An Egyptian portrait Head of Amenhotep III
basalt
circa 1390-1380 B.C.
6¼ in. (15.9 cm.) high
London, 7 December 1994, £65,300 ($101,998)

This rare Egyptian portrait head of Amenhotep III, previously unpublished, shows the youth and sensuality of the young king who, as a teenager, ascended his father Tuthmosis IV's throne in circa 1391 B.C. He inherited a wealthy country with an empire stretching from Nubia to Syria. During his fairly peaceful thirty-eight year reign he embarked on an extensive campaign of building monuments and commissioning statuary. One of his epithets was 'the Dazzling Sun Disk of all lands'. In this head, full of vitality, can perhaps also be seen the youthful features of Amenhotep IV (Akhenaten) and Tutankhamun.

*Right:*
An Egyptian Face of a Pharaoh,
perhaps Amenhotep I
limestone
New Kingdom, Dynasty XVIII, 1550-1307 B.C.
7⅜ in. (18.7 cm.) high
New York, 2 June 1995, $51,700 (£32,344)

*Far right:*
An Egyptian Bust of a Woman
greywacke
Ptolemaic period, 304-30 B.C.
6⅞ in. (17.5 cm.) high
New York, 15 December 1994,
$29,900 (£19,167)

The hieroglyphic text on the back tells us that
she was 'the beneficiary of the funerary
offerings bestowed upon her by the Theban
triad of Amun, Mut, and Khonsu, as well as by
Osiris and Isis'.

A Roman Bust of Antinous
marble
circa 130-138 A.D., with an 18th Century
*nemes* headdress
23⅝ in. (60 cm.) high
Sold from the collection of the
Earl of Shelburne
London, 5 July 1995, £47,700 ($76,320)

Antinous was the Emperor Hadrian's favourite.
The importance of the Lansdowne Antinous
lies in the fact that it was part of the Emperor's
own collection of commissioned statues of his
acolyte which was housed in his famous Villa
at Tivoli; the provenance is direct and
documented following its excavation by
Gavin Hamilton at Tivoli in 1769. The head
also admirably reflects the eighteenth-century
taste for embellishing ancient sculpture with
sympathetic restorations. In this case the
additional Egyptian headdress was probably
worked in Cavaceppi's studio in Rome prior to
the bust being dispatched to Lord Shelburne
in 1772.

An East Greek 'Plastic' Vase, in the form of
a dead Hare
circa late 7th Century B.C.
8⅝ in. (21.9 cm.) long
New York, 2 June 1995,
$55,200 (£34,500)

A Hellenistic Lotus Bowl
silver-gilt
2nd Century B.C.
4¼ in. (10.8 cm.) high;
8¾ in. (22.3 cm.) diameter
London, 7 December 1995,
£56,500 ($88,253)

Attributed to the CHAIRE PAINTER
An Attic red-figure Pyxis
490-480 B.C.
2⅞ in. (7.3 cm.) high;
4½ in. (11.4 cm.) diameter
London, 5 July 1995,
£76,300 ($122,080)

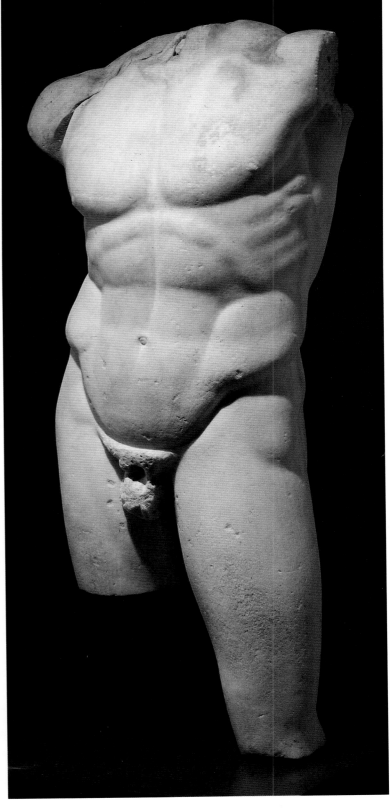

A Roman Bust of the philosopher Metrodoros
marble
circa 2nd Century A.D.
18¾ in. (47.6 cm.) high
New York, 2 June 1995, $134,500 (£84,062)

A Roman Torso of the *Diadumenos* of Polykleitos
marble
circa 1st Century A.D., after the original of circa 430 B.C.
44⅛ in. (112 cm.) high
Sold by the Rudolf Nureyev Dance Foundation
New York, 13 January 1995, $310,500 (£211,140)

Ferdowsi (d. 1020):
Shahnameh, with 22 miniatures
(part frontispiece illustrated)
Shiraz, Persia, circa 1570
folio 17½ x 11½ in.
(44.5 x 29.1 cm.)
text 11¼ x 7 in. (28.6 x 17.8 cm.)
London, 25 April 1995,
£402,300 ($643,680)

The Shahnameh (literally 'book of kings') is probably the most popular single work of Persian literature. Written by the poet Ferdowsi in about the year 1000, it recounts in one seamless development the history of Persia from the beginning of mankind when the first king encouraged his people to wear clothes while his successor invented fire, through a series of lengthy battles between Iran and its mythical neighbour, Turan, continuing on to Alexander the Great, and ending up with the fully historical Sassanian dynasty who ruled Iran in the first few centuries of the first milennium A.D. until the Moslem conquest. The book became very popular in the Safavid period (1501-1722 A.D.), when the rulers used it to emphasise their long tradition of kingship. Many magnificent copies were created for rulers and nobles of the time. The present copy was produced in the South Persian city of Shiraz, traditionally famed for its poets and love of the arts.

*Top left:*
Flight from Attack, a miniature from
the British Library/Chester Beatty *Akbarnameh*
Mughal India, circa 1602
miniature 9 x 5¼ in. (22.9 x 13.3 cm.)
leaf 13¼ x 8½ in. (33.8 x 22.2 cm.)
London, 25 April 1995, £49,935 ($79,896)

*Top right:*
Eight Leaves of Calligraphy (one illustrated)
four signed by Sultan Muhammad Nur
Herat, Persia, 16th Century
folio 14 x 19 in. (35.4 x 23.3 cm.)
London, 25 April 1995,
£35,287 ($56,459)

*Above:*
A lacquer Binding
Persia or Turkey,
first half 16th Century
each board 12¾ x 8 in. (32.3 x 20.5 cm.)
London, 18 October 1994,
£28,750 ($46,287)

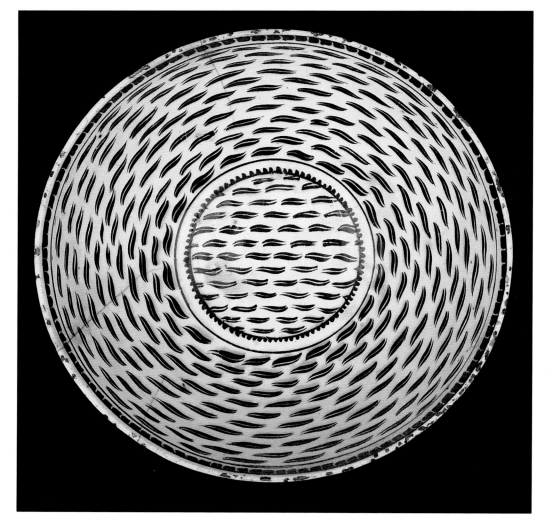

*Right, clockwise from top left:*
A Western Anatolian Star Carpet
(detail illustrated)
early 16th Century
18 ft. 4 in. x 7 ft. 8 in. (557 cm. x 234 cm.)
London, 20 October 1994,
£106,000 ($171,720)

An Ottoman Cairene Carpet
(detail illustrated)
Cairo, Egypt, 16th Century
23 ft. 5 in. x 10 ft. 11 in. (714 cm. x 333 cm.)
New York, 16 December 1994,
$123,500 (£79,167)

ZAREH PENYAMIN
(Turkish Armenian 1890-1949)
A silk and metal thread Koum Kapi Carpet
(detail illustrated)
Istanbul, Turkey, first quarter 20th Century
9 ft. 10 in. x 6 ft. 8 in. (299 cm. x 204 cm.)
London, 20 October 1994,
£133,500 ($216,270)

*Top:*
An inscribed jade Bowl
Central Asia, 1397-8 A.D., 4¾ in. (12 cm.) diameter
London, 25 April 1995, £25,877 ($41,403)

This bowl was made for the Amir Timur (Timur-leng or Tamerlane in literature) as is established by its inscription. Timur's conquests from 1370 until his death in 1405 were modelled on those of Ghengis Khan, encompassing almost as great an empire as his predecessor's. He combined extreme ruthlessness, and in some cases cruelty, with a great love of the arts.

*Above:*
An Iznik hemispherical Bowl
circa 1540
12½ in. (31.9 cm.) diameter
London, 25 April, 1995,
£25,877 ($41,403)

A Safavid silk and metal thread 'Polonaise' Carpet
Persia, probably Isfahan, early 17th Century
14 ft. x 5 ft. 9 in. (427 x 175 cm.)
London, 20 October 1994, £419,500 ($679,590)

One of the features most commented on by
seventeenth-century European travellers to the
Persian cities of Kashan and Isfahan was their
sumptuous weaving. Particularly rarified to the
European eye were those in silk and metal thread.
These carpets, which earned the misnomer
'Polonaise' through an incorrect early exhibition
catalogue entry, usually have fields of silver and
gold thread finely wound around silk filaments,
while the piled designs are executed in many
brilliant shades of silk. Their popularity with
Europeans meant that they were often used as
diplomatic gifts by the Persians. Others were found
as a highly prized item of commerce. About three
hundred have survived. Of these, almost all of
known provenance have come through one or
another of the noble or royal houses of Europe.

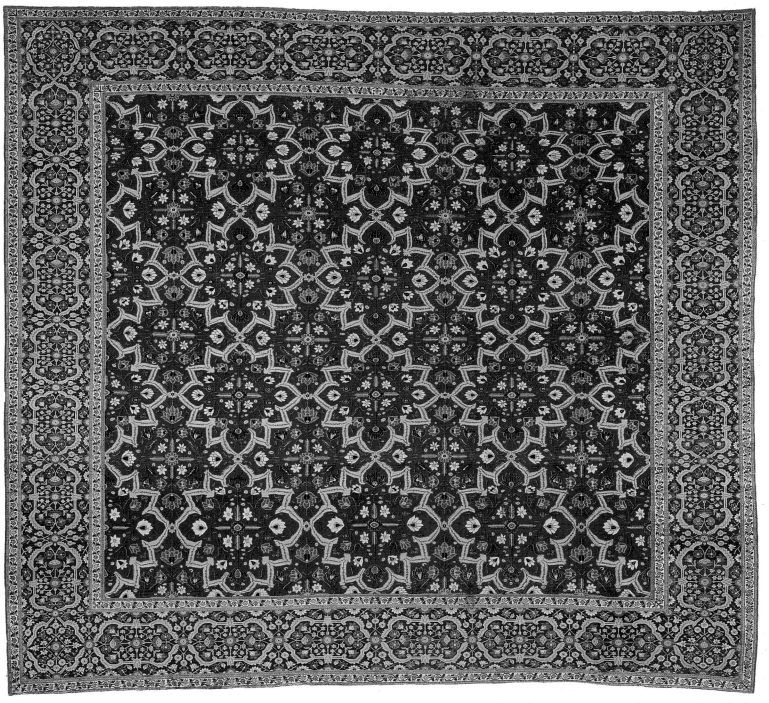

A Mughal millefleur 'Star-Lattice' Carpet
North India, late 17th-early 18th Century
New York, 10 April 1995, $992,500 (£620,313)
A world record price for an Oriental carpet at auction

This is one of twelve known Mughal carpets identified as the 'Millefleur' group because of a shared design repertoire of intricately-drawn floral vinery and the use of the finest materials, such as Pashmina wool. The superlative quality of this group of carpets, suggests that these were probably woven for the Mughal Court or high-ranking members of the Indian aristocracy.

The noble status of the present carpet was recognized by early collectors and it was acquired by Cornelius Vanderbilt II in the 1880s for his spectacular New York City mansion, 1 West 57th Street. Vanderbilt later moved the carpet to a prominent place in the master bedroom at 'The Breakers', his country palace at Newport, Rhode Island. The carpet remained in the Vanderbilt family's possession for nearly a hundred years, which helps to explain the exceptionally well-preserved condition that allows us to experience the splendour of Mughal carpet weaving as originally intended.

A slip-decorated Dingyao Baluster Vase, *Meiping*
Northern Song Dynasty (960-1127)
12¼ in. (31.2 cm.) high
Hong Kong, 31 October 1994, H.K.$9,700,000 (£772,908)

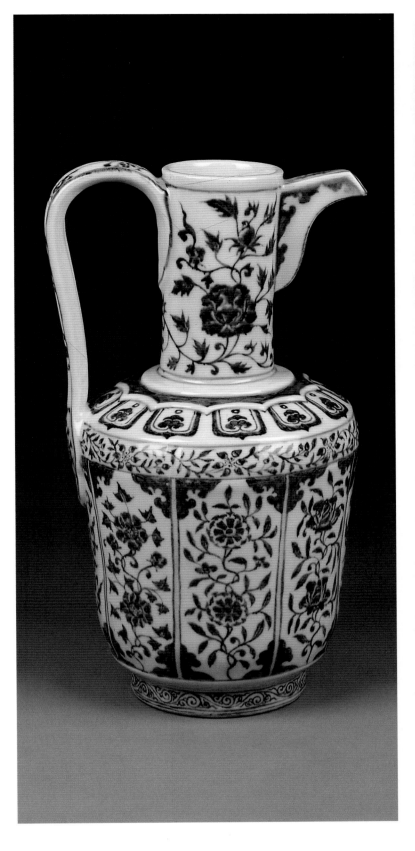

A blue and white Ewer, *Zhi Hu*
Ming Dynasty, Yongle (1403-24)
14⅜ in. (36.5 cm.) high
Hong Kong, 31 October 1994, H.K.$8,820,000 (£702,789)

*Top:*
An underglaze-red-decorated *Kendi*
Ming Dynasty, Hongwu (1368-98)
6 in. (15.2 cm.) high
Sold from the Arthur M. Sackler Collections
New York, 1 December 1994, $420,500 (£267,516)

A small underglaze-red-decorated Ewer
Ming Dynasty, Hongwu (1368-98)
4⅟₁₆ in. (10.3 cm.) high
Sold from the Scheinman Collection
New York, 23 March 1995, $112,500 (£70,755)

A *doucai* Moonflask
Qianlong seal mark and of the period (1736-95)
20 in. (51 cm.) high
Hong Kong, 1 May 1995, H.K.$8,160,000 (£654,896)

A black-ground green-glazed Dish
Qianlong seal mark and of the period (1736-95)
18⅞ in. (48 cm.) diameter
London, 5 June 1995, £331,500 ($526,090)

# THE DIANA CARGO

## by Colin D. Sheaf

This year saw a fourth great shipwrecked cargo of Chinese export porcelain come to auction at Christie's Amsterdam. Each cargo has brought its own challenges. The cargo of the ship 'Diana', trading between India and Canton, sank in March 1817, with an extensive commercial cargo of Chinese manufactures that included the 24,000 pieces of porcelain offered in this auction. The fashionable retail emporia of Anglo-Indian Madras would certainly have welcomed this arrival of chic enamelled or blue and white porcelain which had sadly disappeared one night in the Straits of Malacca. Could the owners, the Government of Malaysia in association with Malaysian Historical Salvors (MHS), expect Western buyers today to show the same enthusiasm?

The 'Diana' project had one crucial element to appeal to a buying public fascinated by the historical romance of a lost ship. This was the wealth of archival material about the boat, laboriously assembled over a decade by Managing Director of MHS, Dorian Ball. But the 'Diana's' history still required an imaginative presentation, and the porcelain needed to be set successfully into an auction context. This was the primary objective which fifteen years of shipwreck experience, and an extensive database of likely buyers, made Christie's uniquely well placed to attain. The Cargo contained some 24,000 pieces of ceramics at the core of the sale, as well as a number of maritime artifacts, and a heavy consignment of partially-dressed marble plaques probably destined for an official edifice in the early British Raj. In all, there were 1,309 lots, bar a small number of representative objects which were retained by private treaty by the Government, for display in the National Museum in Kuala Lumpur.

A pre-sale total estimate of about £1,000,000 set a realistic target. The market for 'Chinese export porcelain' is traditionally narrow, though geographically widespread; and maritime artifacts are not easy to value, since there is no consistent market. But in the event, the two-day six-session sale raised some £2,200,000, with 97% of the lots finding buyers.

The Cargo divided on March 6 and 7 into two clear tastes. More expensive were the collector rarities, notably some of the blue and white porcelain painted with 'Fitzhugh' and 'Canton' designs, long popular in Europe and the United States, which frequently sold for three or four times the estimate. There was also a taste for less sophisticated blue and white porcelain made for export to the markets of South East Asia (and India), which also sold satisfactorily, often doubling the estimate. Since this was traditionally less widely collected, it was especially satisfying that so many new, private bidders registered to acquire the carefully-assembled sets of saucer dishes or bowls, available in multiples of twelve, up to services able to accommodate 48 users.

The auction attracted extensive publicity. Innovations this time included more extensive video film circulation in the United States, coupled with a 'Satellite media' tour there for Dorian Ball which hit 120 markets with 315 'airings' of the 'Diana' story; and live prime-time radio interviews. In the United Kingdom, a 'readers' competition' in the Sunday Express attracted a huge response. Special exhibitions were mounted in London, Glasgow and Brussels; and a 'whistle-stop' bus tour to museum venues around Holland attracted an unprecedented number of visitors. Appearances by Dorian Ball and Christie's expert staff on many of the world's major television and satellite networks ensured that the momentum was maintained until the sale. A group of senior Malaysian Government officials, representing the Ministry of Finance and cultural divisions including the National Museum, joined the Malaysian Ambassador to the Netherlands at formal receptions, culminating with a gala dinner, where 'Diana' porcelain researchers, salvors and collectors happily mixed, before the auction provided a fitting finale to a project which attracted worldwide attention.

A 'Collector's Cabinet'
of Diana Merchandise
circa 1816
Amsterdam, 7 March 1995,
Fl.6,325 (£2,530)

*Top left:*
A carved white jade Pendant of a female Dancer
Warring States Period (475-221 B.C.)
3¼ in. (8.3 cm.) high
Sold from the Arthur M. Sackler Collections
New York, 1 December 1994, $299,500 (£190,764)

*Top right:*
An Imperial faceted small transparent *Xi Hu Shui* glass Bottle
Qianlong period (1736-95)
1⅜ in. (3.5 cm.) high and across
New York, 23 March 1995, $107,000 (£67,296)

*Above:*
An inscribed rhinoceros horn quatrefoil Tray
Ming Dynasty (1368-1644)
6¼ in. (16 cm.) long
Sold from the Arthur M. Sackler Collections
New York, 1 December 1994, $189,500 (£120,701)

A polychrome wood Figure of Guanyin
Jin Dynasty (1115-1234)
50½ in. (128.2 cm.) high
Hong Kong, 30 October 1994, H.K.$3,210,000 (£255,777)

WEN ZHENGMING (1470-1559)
Scholars Meeting: The Study by old Trees
Hanging scroll, ink on paper
20⅝ x 12⁵⁄₁₆ in. (52.4 x 31.3 cm.)
Hong Kong, 30 October 1994, H.K.$1,670,000 (£133,068)

XU GU (1824-1896)
Peaches, Loquats, Pine, Plum Blossom and Lily
(Peaches illustrated)
A set of four hanging scrolls, ink and colour on paper
each measuring 48⅝ x 11⅞ in. (123.6 x 30 cm.)
Hong Kong, 30 October 1994, H.K.$1,890,000 (£150,598)

# KOREAN ART

An inlaid Celadon *Maebyong*
Koryo Dynasty, 12th Century
11⅜ in. (29 cm.) high
New York, 25 October 1994,
$794,500 (£484,645)

This superb example of a Koryo dynasty (918-1392) inlaid celadon bottle-vase (*maebyong*) was sold in New York. Korean potters were achieving beautiful celadon glazes by the first half of the twelfth century. The earliest appearance of the inlay *sanggam* technique has been the subject of controversy but there is general agreement that the technique reached maturity by the second half of the twelfth century. The inlaid pattern is incised on the unfired body and the incised areas are then filled with white or iron slip.

The stately and elegant designs on four sides of the bottle are restrained yet rhythmic at the same time. Cranes stand at the base of elaborate clusters of bamboo and flowering white blossoms. While the Koryo *maebyong* originated under the influence of Chinese models, the swelling S-curve of the vase is a shape distinctive to Korean vases.

*Right:*
An iron-decorated large Jar
Choson Dynasty, 16th-17th Century
7⅛ in. (18.1 cm.) high
New York, 25 October 1994,
$552,500 (£337,025)

An hexagonal blue and white Brush Holder
Choson Dynasty, 18th Century
4⅞ in. (12.5 cm.) high
New York, 26 April 1995,
$1,025,500 (£635,810)

A blue and white five-clawed Dragon Jar
Choson Dynasty, 18th Century
20¾ in. (52.5 cm.) high
New York, 26 April 1995, $1,652,500 (£1,024,550)

Five-clawed dragons striding through clouds in pursuit of a flaming pearl are often found as decoration on Ming and Qing imperial porcelains. In Korea they are likewise associated exclusively with the court. They are royal insignia emblematic of power and dignity. Jars of this unusually large size and fine quality are extremely rare and were probably used for formal court ceremonies.

Owing to the difficulties encountered by Korean potters when manufacturing pieces of such a large size, surviving jars of this type are frequently mis-fired or mis-shapen. Fortunately in this case there were no problems with either the shape or the surface, or the condition. The high price we achieved, therefore, came as no surprise.

An early enamelled Kakiemon Vase
late 17th Century
10¼ in. (26 cm.) high
London, 15 November 1994, £62,000 ($98,456)

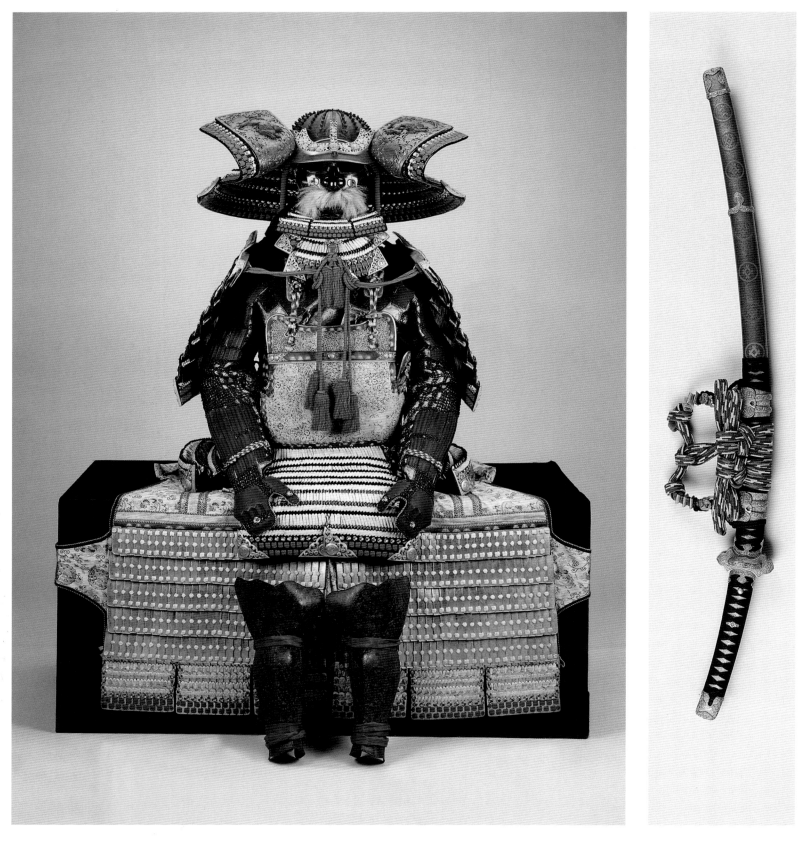

*Above left:*
A white laced *O-Yoroi*
Armour, Meiji period (1868-1912);
Helmet Bowl, late Kamakura period,
early 14th Century; Shinguards, 17th Century
London, 14 November 1994,
£47,700 ($75,747)

*Above right:*
An *Efu Tachi Koshirae*
Edo period, late 18th Century
the blade 25½ in. (64.5 cm.) long
London, 20 June 1995, £34,500 ($55,304)

*Right, clockwise from top left:*
TOMOTADA
An ivory Netsuke of a Tigress
signed 'Tomotada', late 18th Century
1½ in. (4 cm. high)
London, 28 March 1995, £9,200 ($14,720)

YOSHINAGA
An ivory Netsuke
signed 'Yoshinaga'
Edo period, late 18th Century
3½ in. (9 cm.) high
New York, 26 April 1995, $63,000 (£39,060)

GOTO ICHIJO (1791-1876)
A *shakudo daisho Tsuba*
signed 'Goto Hokyo Ichijo' and *Kao*
late Edo period, circa 1860
3⅛ x 3 in. (8.0 cm. and 7.5 cm.)
London, 28 March 1995,
£17,250 ($27,600)

An ivory Netsuke of a *Karako*
18th Century
4⅛ in. (10.3 cm.) high
London, 23 June 1995, £18,400 ($29,440)

# THE LAWRENCE BICKFORD COLLECTION OF JAPANESE WRESTLER PRINTS

## by Sebastian Izzard

Christie's first sale of Japanese sporting memorabilia was an unprecedented success. Now that the great Sumo wrestling bouts appear on late-night satellite television and demonstration tourneys are held throughout the world, with the wrestlers themselves promoting products ranging from mattresses and *tatami* mats to beer and other sundries, the sport has gained an international status, especially since non-Japanese wrestlers have shown that they can compete at the highest levels of the sport. The arcane rules and regulations have become familiar to us, as has the pageantry and ceremony of the tournaments.

In October 1994 Christie's New York offered the unique Sumo print collection of Lawrence Bickford, a scientist who arrived in Japan in 1964 on an assignment to establish a research laboratory in Tokyo. An accidental purchase of a well-weathered Sumo triptych led to a collection, assembled over a period of thirty years, that evolved into the most significant and comprehensive ever held in private hands.

Although Sumo wrestling in one form or another has been an integral part of Japanese life for at least a thousand years – Sumo is one of the world's earliest surviving professional sports – it was not until the second half of the eighteenth century that heroic portraits of the great wrestlers became popular in Edo (the modern Tokyo) and developed into a distinctive genre of *ukiyo-e* (pictures of the floating world). Earlier the sport was associated with Kyoto and Osaka, and when individual wrestlers appeared in prints it was as curiosities rather than as celebrated personalities.

By the late eighteenth century Edo had begun to supplant Osaka as the main centre of the sport. An unbroken string of sixty-three victories by the leading wrestler Tanikaze Kajinosuke was ended with a sensational upset by the young Onogawa Kisaburo of Osaka. This series of fights raised public interest to fever pitch and provided Katsukawa Shunsho (1726-1792), who specialised in realistic portraits of actors, with the opportunity to design a series of luxurious prints featuring pairs of leading wrestlers in the ring. He portrayed them wearing decorated aprons, often emblazoned with their names, in the formal ceremonies preceding the actual bouts. The commerical success of these prints was such that the publisher commissioned another set, of double size, which featured the actual bouts. A vigorous new genre of Japanese prints had been born.

Wrestlers were quickly raised to equal status with the leading actors and popular beauties who provided the main subjects of Japanese prints. Such was public demand that Shunsho and the artists who followed him quickly took the wrestlers out of the ring and began to show them in their street clothes picnicking, relaxing in the brothel district, in their dressing rooms, or merely strolling in the city.

The Katsukawa school dominated the genre in the late eighteenth and early nineteenth century, but soon after the 1820s leadership passed to Utagawa Kunisada (1786-1865), of the rival Utagawa school. Kunisada's dynamic portraits of wrestlers, printed with vibrant mineral pigments that came into use during the 1830s and 1840s, have a Pop-Art quality that proved especially popular. The massive figures of the wrestlers appear to burst from the surface of the paper.

As the nineteenth century waned, Sumo prints were replaced by photographs publicising the bouts. Only the relationship between the sport and Shinto rites, which ensured imperial backing, provided new subject matter in the form of views of the emperor Meiji attending wrestling matches (a match was performed in his honour in the grounds of one of the imperial estates in March 1884). The imperial patronage guaranteed official sponsorship in the pre-World War II period. It was the American Occupation that brought wrestlers from Samoa and Hawaii to Japan and contributed to the international popularity of Sumo today.

This popularity ensured a positive response to Dr Bickford's collection. The preview exhibition in Tokyo was crowded with print enthusiasts, museum curators, members of families associated with Sumo, and dealers. The preview in New York was similarly well attended, and on the day of the auction the room was packed.

Kitagawa Utamaro (1754-1806) is best known for his prints of beautiful women. His humorous print of Tanikaze Kajinosuke neck-wrestling with Kintaro, the legendary Strong Boy, observed by the three great beauties of the period – Okita, the waitress of the Naniwaya teashop, Toyohina, the daughter of the famous raconteur Tomimoto Buzendayu II acting as judge, and Ohisa of the Takashimaya emporium – provided the high point of the sale. Estimated at $8,000-10,000 the bidding quickly escalated and ended with a duel between a dealer in the room and a bidder on the telephone. The telephone bidder won with a bid of $80,000, ten times the low estimate. By the time the sale was complete 93 percent of the lots had been sold for a total of $644,341.

KITAGAWA UTAMARO (1754-1806), *dai oban yoko-e*
signed 'Utamaro ga', 14 x 17 in. (35.6 x 43.4 cm.)
Sold from the Bickford Collection
New York, 25 October 1994, $90,500 (£55,205)

SHARAKU (active 1794-95)
*oban tate-e*, an *okubi-e* portrait of the actor Sakata Hangoro III in the role of the villain Fujikawa
Mizuemon, signed 'Toshusai Sharaku ga'
15 x 10 in. (38 x 25.3 cm.). New York, 26 April 1995, $332,500 (£206,150)

ANONYMOUS, 17th Century
The Arrival of the Southern Barbarians (detail)
Six-panel screen, ink, colour, gold pigment and gold leaf on
paper, mounted on brocade
5 ft. 6 in. x 11 ft. 5 in. (167.8 x 346.2 cm.)
New York, 25 October 1994, $662,500 (£404,125)

This is the left-hand screen of a pair depicting the arrival of
Portuguese traders at Nagasaki on the west coast of Kyushu, the
southernmost of the four main islands of Japan. The Portuguese
*nao do trato* was known to the Japanese as the *kurofune* (black ship)
or *Namban Bune* ('Namban' ship), the ship of the southern
barbarians. The great ship was a three-deck carrack of up to 1,600
tons, and its enormous size was the cause of much wonder and
excitement in Japan at the time of its annual visit. (This particular
ship has been embellished by the artist with some distinctly
orientalizing features.) The crew is here shown performing
alarming acrobatic feats in the rigging as they dismantle the sails.
Cargo is already being offloaded onto the shore and curious
sightseers have hired a small craft for a closer look at the great
ship. The admiring Japanese would have been shocked by the
words of an experienced European traveller who said 'The ships
are mightly foul and stink withal.'

The carrack set off for Macao and Japan from Goa, the centre
of the Portuguese empire in Asia, and many of the crew were
natives of the Indian subcontinent. Portuguese ships were
permitted access to Japan between 1571 and 1640, until the Shogun
put into effect a seclusionist policy that closed the country to
all outsiders other than Chinese merchants, a handful of Dutch
traders, and occasional Korean emissaries.

The European captain-major has been ferried ashore. He is
shown parading through town at the far right edge of the
screen, wearing an elegant red cloak, and followed by various
attendants, one of whom carries a furled sunshade. The now
missing right-hand screen probably depicted a continuation of the
shop fronts lining the main street and a small welcoming
committee of Jesuits from the local Catholic mission, coming
out to meet the traders.

The earliest screen of this type is thought to date from the 1590s
and is attributed to Kano Mitsunobu, who was called from Kyoto
to the city of Nagoya in northern Kyushu, where he observed the
Portuguese at first hand. The exotic subject fascinated the Japanese,
and it was copied in numerous versions in the seventeenth century
by artists in Kyoto for a clientèle curious to study the strange
costumes and odd physiognomy of these entertaining southern
barbarians. The artist typically exaggerates their height and
emphasizes the balloon-like bagginess of their *bombacha* pantaloons,
but also focuses on distinctive details such as the large handkerchiefs
and heavy gold necklaces.

*Top:*

KAWAI GYOKUDO (Japanese, 1873-1957)
*Ayutsuri* Fishing for *ayu*
signed 'Gyokudo' and sealed
ink and colour on silk, 18¼ x 22½ in. (46.5 x 57.4 cm.)
Sold from the Estate of Ralph E. Phillips and Dorothy W. Phillips
New York, 25 October 1994, $90,500 (£55,521)

PARK SOO-GUN (Korean, 1914-1965)
Country Village
signed 'Soo-Gun'
oil on board
11½ x 7 in. (29.2 x 17.8 cm.)
New York, 25 October 1994, $266,500 (£162,565)

# TRIBAL ART

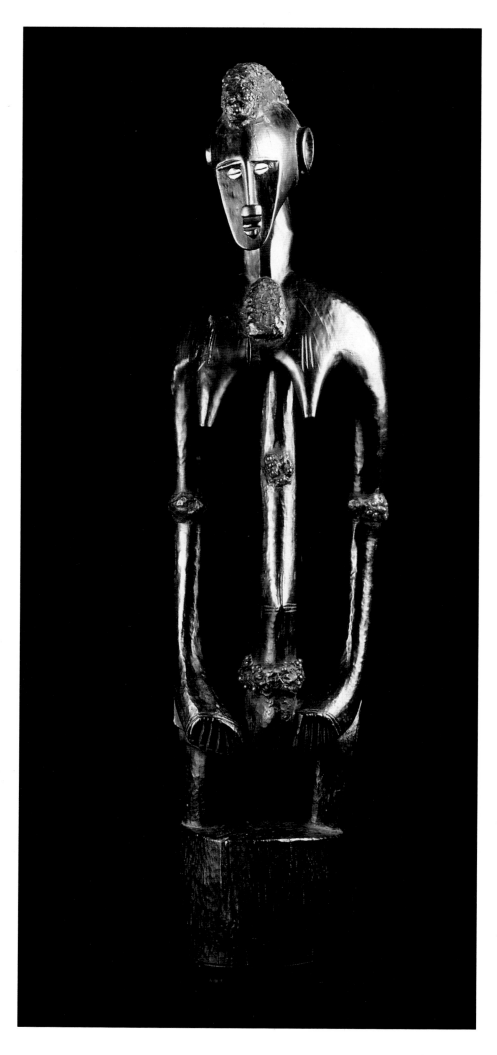

A Senufo female Rhythm Pounder, *Pombilele*
Northern Senufo Area, Ivory Coast
36 in. (91 cm.) high
Sold from the collection of the late
Ambassador William A.M. Burden,
formerly in the collection of Helena Rubinstein
New York, 5 May 1995, $1,212,500 (£763,875)

*Right, clockwise from top left:*
An Algonquian Bowl
North America, possibly 18th Century
8¼ in. (20.9 cm.) wide
New York, 8 June 1995, $90,500 (£57,015)

A Lorette-Huron quilled skin Pouch
Canada, circa 1830
7⅞ in. (20 cm.) wide
London, 26 June 1995, £36,700 ($58,720)

Part of a group from the acting cupboard at
Overbury Court, Gloucestershire, which sold for
a total of £96,787 ($154,859).

A Solomon Islands inlaid ceremonial Shield
Santa Isabel, circa 1840
30¾ in. (78.1 cm.) high
New York, 5 May 1995, $211,500 (£133,245)

A Chokwe Mask, *Mwana Pwo*
Mwangambe Kingdom, Angola
8⅝ in. (22 cm.) high
London, 30 November 1994, £51,000 ($79,560)

# PRINTED BOOKS AND MANUSCRIPTS

## *EMPEROR OTTO III'S PRAYERBOOK AND JOHN EVELYN'S DIARY: TWO PRIVATE-TREATY SALES OF LITERARY PROPERTY*

### *by Felix de Marez Oyens*

In addition to auctioning fine libraries, Christie's have always actively sold individual manuscripts and whole archives by private treaty. This discreet method serves our clients particularly well when we offer medieval or autograph manuscripts of unique national importance, but provincial archives destined for local record offices can also benefit from avoiding the glare of the saleroom. Arguing values and negotiations about price often demand considerable patience from all parties and their agents; nevertheless, when we deal with willing buyers as well as represent willing sellers, failure is an extremely rare occurrence. The advantages to the seller of taking this course often relate to his tax position, sometimes also to the laws governing the export of illuminated manuscripts or historical papers from their country of origin. The gain to the buyer may be to escape open-market competition and, thus, to safeguard for the nation manuscripts that have eluded public ownership for centuries.

Two of the most significant literary sales ever made in this way were concluded during the 1994-95 season. The first was a late-tenth-century illuminated manuscript negotiated by Christie's on behalf of Count Schönborn, owner of the matchless private library at the Summer Castle of Pommersfelden, to the Bavarian State Library in Munich; purchased with the help from – among other federal and state bodies – the Kulturstiftung der Länder, at DM 7.4 million (apparently the fourth-highest price ever realised for a single book), Otto III's prayerbook has been described in the press announcement issued by the Bayerische Staatsbibliothek as their most important acquisition since secularization of the monastic collections in South-German lands in 1803. The second was John Evelyn's archive, which has been called by representatives of the British Library their most important acquisition of the last decade among such major other seventeenth-century additions as the Coke, Trumbull and Petty Papers; the most famous manuscript in this outstanding archive, completely and no doubt definitively published by E. S. de Beer in 1955, is Evelyn's autograph Diary, which by itself accounted for almost half of the total price paid (with the financial assistance from the National Heritage Memorial Fund). Acting for the late Major Peter Evelyn's Will Trustees, Christie's approached the British Library, who were advised by Bernard Quaritch Ltd. A dozen and a half years earlier the Library's agents had already bought at a series of Christie's auction sales most of the printed books from Evelyn's library that were annotated by the Diarist himself.

When manuscripts have been in the same hands and particularly in the same place for hundreds of years, a sudden change of ownership for whatever reason is sometimes regretted. However, there is nothing like a major financial transaction to spur the study of artistic or literary monuments. Both these private sales handled by Christie's have prompted the publication of illustrated scholarly accounts. During the last eight years the Kulturstiftung der Länder under the directorship of Dr. Klaus Maurice has not only helped German museums and libraries acquire art and literature of national

importance – quite apart from making German culture more accessible abroad, for instance by supporting the British Library in its acquisition of the Todd-Bowden Collection of Tauchnitz editions and by subsidizing the Bodleian Library's programme of cataloguing its incunabula – it has also commissioned monographs in order to document each purchase or project. This well produced series called *Patrimonia* now consists of more than a hundred issues and forms a worthy record of the Stiftung's valuable work. Number 84 is published under the title *Gebetbuch Ottos III. Clm 301111* [the Bavarian State Library's pressmark] and contains two main contributions: 'Kaiser Otto III.' by Knut Görich, an introduction to the political, military and religious conditions prevailing during Otto's tragically short life (980-1002) and reign (elected King in 983, regency of his mother Theophanu until 991 and of his grandmother Adelheid until 994, crowned Emperor at Rome by Pope Gregory V in 996); and 'Das Gebetbuch Ottos III.' by Elisabeth Klemm, an excellent analysis of the textual contents of this small – and now slightly imperfect – private prayerbook, of its iconography, the Byzantine-Italian influence evident in the miniatures, its origin in Mainz and its approximate date (985). Probably commissioned for the child king by Archbishop Willigis and Empress Theophanu, written in gold on purple vellum and illustrated with five miniatures, Otto III's manuscript as a book of private devotion stands alone in importance and rarity with the even more celebrated and much earlier illuminated prayerbook for Charles the Bald (d.877), its near-neighbour in Munich's Schatzkammer der Residenz. Otto himself is depicted three times in the miniatures, a unique feature. Nothing is known about the later provenance of the codex, not even exactly when or how it entered the library at Pommersfelden. It presumably belonged to the Schönborns since the eighteenth century, but there is no evidence that it was bought by the greatest collector of the family, Prince Elector Lothar Franz (1655-1729). To celebrate their acquisition the manuscript curators of the Bavarian State Library built an astonishing exhibition around the Prayerbook of early Ottonian book illumination and treasure bindings, including two Sacramentaries, two Gospel Books from Reichenau (one bound in an ivory bookcover for Theophanu), two other liturgical manuscripts from Regensburg, and Byzantine and Lorraine ivory bookcovers, all tenth or eleventh-century and all from the Library's own holdings!

Christie's offer for sale of Evelyn's large archive undoubtedly inspired more complete and intense study of his papers – with the exception of the Diary – than they had ever received before. Yet, for the last forty years the archive had been placed on deposit by the Evelyn family at Christ Church, Oxford, where it was available to researchers and made accessible through an (unpublished) shelf-list by W. G. Hiscock, deputy librarian and author of several books and articles on Evelyn. After the acquisition was made by the British Library, the editorial board of *The Book Collector* decided that the event was important enough to devote an entire issue of the journal (Summer 1995) to the description of the archive and of the dispersal of Evelyn's printed books eighteen years ago. Theodore Hofmann and Joan Winterkorn of Quaritch and Frances Harris and Hilton Kelliher of the British Library base their article, ' John Evelyn's Archive at the British Library', on reports they had written during the negotiations. Nicolas Barker, former conservator at the British Library and editor of *The Book Collector* for more than a quarter of a century, describes in 'The Sale of the Evelyn Library, 1977-78' the controversies surrounding the auctions of the printed books and the strategies employed by the British Library to save for the nation as many books with autograph annotations by Evelyn as possible; finally, in 'The British Library and the Library of John Evelyn' Michael Hunter of Birbeck College, University of London, gives a short account of Evelyn's book collecting and of the losses sustained by his library prior to the Christie's sales, and supplies an 'Alphabetical list of the books from John Evelyn's library now in the British Library'. Evelyn's so-called Diary (covering the entire period of his life, 1620-1706, written from circa 1660 onwards) is rightly considered a uniquely important document of English cultural life in the seventeenth century, but his voluminous other papers on art, economics, farming, horticulture, medicine, philosophy, politics, scientific experiments, and theology, and his autograph poetry and translations from the classics, as well as his correspondence with an extensive array of luminaries in public life, scholars and *littérateurs,* are no less fascinating and reflect his immense energy, wide interest in learning, virtuosity and wit, which were recognised by his fellow diarist, Samuel Pepys.

If the Codex Leicester proves that unique opportunities for the private collector still occur in the saleroom, Otto III's Prayerbook and Evelyn's Diary show that great research libraries can quietly continue to collect. Christie's are pleased to play their role in both markets.

*Above right:*
King Otto III receiving his Prayerbook
dedication miniature at the end of
Otto III's Prayerbook
illuminated manuscript on vellum
Mainz, c. 985
Sold by private treaty, 1994
Reproduced by courtesy of the Bayerische
Staatsbibliothek

*Right:*
John Evelyn's autograph Diary
*Kalendarium* [de Beer's MS. K]
quarto, two volumes, c. 1660-1706
with his later autograph revision:
*De vita propria* [de Beer's MS. V]
bound for the author in gold-tooled armorial
morocco
Sold by private treaty as part of the complete
archive, 1995
Reproduced by courtesy of the British
Library Board

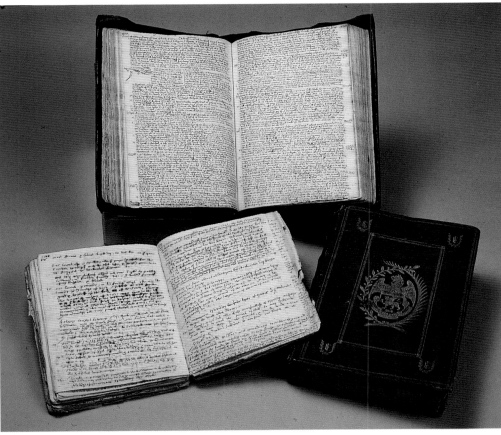

*Above:*
The Prayerbook of Countess Dorothea von Mansfeld,
in German, by the scribe S.B. and dated 1551
Illuminated manuscript on vellum, with 30 miniatures
(two signed by the artist S.G.)
8⅛ x 5⅞ in. (20.5 x 15 cm.)
Sold from the collection of the late Dr. Sali Guggenheim of Zurich
London, 28 June 1995, £265,500 ($418,959)

This fine artist of the school of Hans Sebald Beham was possibly
Sebastian Glockendon of Nuremberg. The patroness appears in the
final miniature and her coat-of-arms at the beginning. Important
German illuminated manuscripts of the mid-sixteenth century are of
the greatest rarity.

*Right, from top:*
Gerard Mercator (1512-1594) & Jodocus Hondius (1563-1611)
*Atlas*, in French, Amsterdam: 1619
Large folio 18½ x 12½ in. (46.7 x 31.5 cm.)
158 hand-coloured engraved maps
With two important manuscript maps by the royal engineer and
architect Salomon de Caus (1576-1626) inserted, including a fine
oval world-map, illuminated in gold and colours
From the collection of the 2nd Earl Stanhope (1714-1786)
London, 24 May 1995, £45,500 ($71,435)

JULES VERNE (1828-1905)
*Voyage au centre de la terre* (not after 1864)
Autograph manuscript, 193 pages, from which the first edition was set
New York, 7 October 1994, $266,500 (£167,610)

This is the last manuscript of a major science-fiction novel by Verne
to come on the market.

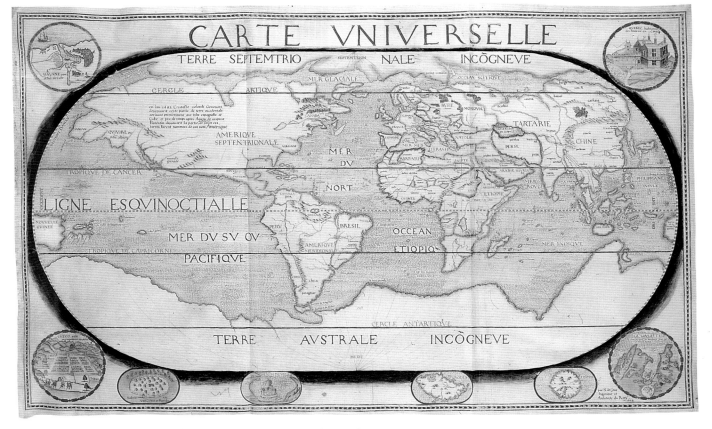

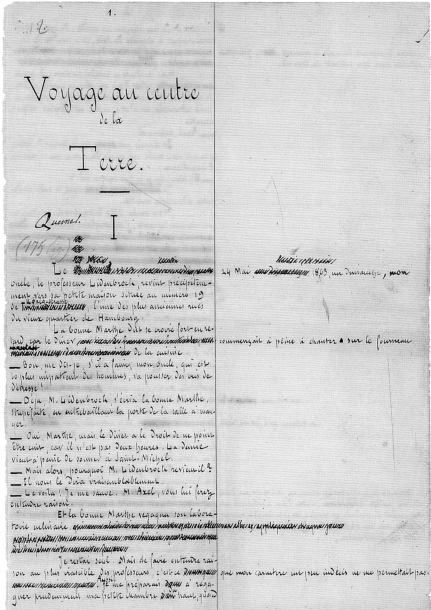

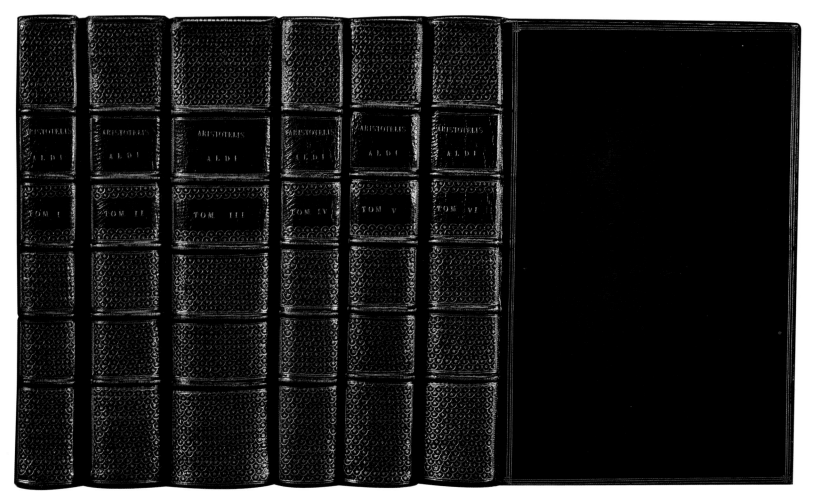

PETRI BEMBI DE AETNA AD
ANGELVM CHABRIELEM
LIBER.

Factum a nobis pueris eft , et quidem fe-
dulo Angele; quod meminiſſe te certo
ſcio;ut fructus ſtudiorum noſtrorum,
quos ferebat illa aetas nõ tam maturos, q̃
uberes,ſemper tibi aliquos promeremus:
nam ſiue dolebas aliquid, ſiue gaudebas;
quae duo ſunt tenerorum animorum ma
xime propriae affectiones; continuo ha-
bebas aliquid a me ,quod legeres,uel gra-
tulationis,uel conſolationis;imbecillum
tu quidem illud,et tenue; ſicuti naſcentia
omnia,et incipientia;ſed tamen quod eſ-
ſet ſatis amplum futurum argumentum
amoris ſummi erga te mei. Verum po-
ſtea,q̃ annis creſcentibus et ſtudia,et iudi
cium increuere ; nóſq; totos tradidimus
graecis magiſtris erudiendos; remiſſiores
paulatim facti ſumus ad ſcribendum, ac
iam etiam minus quotidie audentiores.

**A**

*Above:*
Aristotle (384-322 B.C.)
*Opera*, in Greek
With works by Galen, Theophrastus, Philo Judaeus and others
Edited by Aldus, Thomas Linacre and others
Venice: Aldus Manutius, 1495-8
Super-chancery folio, 12⅛ x 7⅞ in. (30.5 x 20 cm.)
18th Century French green morocco gilt
A fine, complete set from the collections of the
Rev. Henry Drury, Bishop Samuel Butler, Ambroise Firmin-Didot,
Sir Thomas Brooke and Countess Estelle Doheny
New York, 11 November 1994, $288,500 (£180,312)

Pietro Bembo (1470-1547, Cardinal 1539)
*De Aetna*, Venice: Aldus Manutius, February 1495/6
Super-chancery, 8¼ x 6 in. (20.9 x 15 cm.)
First edition and Aldus's first Latin publication
With nine manuscript corrections made in the Aldine shop
London, 3 May 1995, £78,500 ($127,170)

This is arguably the purest example of Renaissance typography,
displaying for the first time the celebrated Roman type cut by
Francesco Griffo, probably the most influential type face in the
history of printing.

Bernhard von Breydenbach (d. 1497)
*Peregrinatio in terram sanctam, in German, Mainz: Erhard Reuwich, 21 June 1486*
Chancery folio, 11¹³⁄₁₆ x 8½ in. (30.1 x 21.5 cm.)
With seven fold-out city views and other woodcuts, all with contemporary hand-colouring.
New York, 19 May 1995, $145,500 (£92,675)

*Above:*
*Preces Christianæ cum parvo officio Beatæ Virginis Mariæ,*
signed by the scribe Nicolas Jarry (c. 1615-1674) and dated 1652
Calligraphic and illuminated manuscript on vellum for Henri de Bullion,
Marquis de Courcy and Seigneur de Fontenay
4⅞ x 3⅛ in. (12.4 x 7.9 cm.)
Contemporary gold-tooled red morocco binding from the Parisian atelier
of Florimond Badier, decorated to a very fine late-fanfare design
From the collections of Gaignat, Count MacCarthy-Reagh, Beckford,
10th Duke of Hamilton, Guyot de Villeneuve, Lebeuf de Montgermont,
Rahir, Schiff and Esmerian
New York, 19 May 1995, $79,500 (£50,636)

*Left:*
Bible, New Testament, in Basque
Translated by J. Leiçarraga from the French Protestant, Geneva version
La Rochelle: Pierre Haultin, 1571
8vo, 6¼ x 4 in. (16.2 x 10.3 cm.)
First edition, of extreme rarity, from the French royal library
Sold by the Mount Stuart Trust
London, 15 March 1995, £166,500 ($264,735)

*Right:*
Bible, in German, Nuremberg: Anton Koberger, 17 February 1483
2 volumes, royal folio 15⅞ x 10⅞ in. (40.3 x 27.7 cm.)
Upwards of 100 woodcuts in contemporary hand-colouring
Contemporary Augsburg binding of blind-stamped calf over wooden boards
Ninth edition of the German Bible, in fine condition
Sold from the Klotz collection
London, 2 November 1994, £58,700 ($96,268)

Der                    Geſchopf                    .V.

Hie hebt ſich an. Geneſis das erſt buch der fünff bucher moyſi. Das erſt Capitel iſt võ der ſchöppfung der werlt vnd aller creaturen. vnd von den wercken der ſechs tag.

 N dem anfang hat got beſchaffen hymel vnd erden. aber dye erde was eytel vnd lere. vnd die vinſternus warn auff dẽ antlitz des abgrunds. vnd der geiſt gots ſwebet oder ward getragen auff dẽ waſſern. Vñ got der ſprach. Es werde dz liecht Vñ das liecht iſt worden. vñ got ſahe dz liecht das es gutt was. vnd er teylet das liecht võ der vinſternus. vnd das liecht hyeß er den tag. vnd die vinſternus die nacht. Vñ es ward abent vñ

morgen eyn tag. Vnd got der ſprach. Es werde das firmament in dem mittel der waſſer. vñ tayle die waſſer võ dẽ waſſern. Vñ got machet das firmament. vnd teylet die waſſer. Dy do waren vnder dem firmament. von dẽ dy do waren ob dem firmament. vnd es iſt alſo geſchehen vnd got hieß das firmament den hymel vnd es iſt der abent vñ der morgẽ der ander tag wordẽ vñ got ſprach aber. Es ſullẽ geſamelt werdẽ dy waſſer. die vnder dem hymel ſeynd. an eyn ſtatt. vñ erſcheyne die durre. vnd es iſt alſo geſchehẽ Vñ got hieß die dürre dz ertreich. Vñ dy ſamnungen der waſſer. hieß er die mere. vnd got ſahe das es was gut. vnd ſprach. Die erde gepere grunend krawt. das do bringe den ſamen. vnd dy öpfelbawm. dz holtz. dz do bringe dy frucht nach ſeym geſchlecht. des ſame ſey in ym ſelbs auff der erde. vnd es iſt alſo geſchehen. vnd die erd bracht grunend kraut. vnd bringenden ſa

# THE LEONARDO DA VINCI CODEX HAMMER

*by Stephen C. Massey and Hope Mayo*

A 72-page autograph manuscript notebook by Leonardo da Vinci (1452-1519) was the prize to be won during a memorable two-minute and thirty-five second auction duel at Christie's New York on 11 November 1994. The victor was Bill Gates, founder and chairman of Microsoft; the vanquished the Italian CARIPLO Foundation, backed by the CARIPLO Bank of Milan. The price, at $30,800,500, is a world record for any item sold at auction other than a painting; and also the highest price achieved in the auction saleroom since the spring of 1990. This achievement now stands tenth in the ranks of the most expensive items sold by a fine art auction house (with all nine paintings ahead of it having sold in the heady days post 1987), and it eclipses the 1983 auction record of £8,140,000 achieved by the Gospels of Henry the Lion, a medieval illuminated manuscript.

The Codex Hammer (so named by its previous owner Dr. Armand Hammer), the only manuscript by Leonardo da Vinci in America, is a lively record of the thoughts of the great Renaissance artist and scientist. Composed of a series of loose sheets on which Leonardo wrote down ideas and observations as they occurred to him, the manuscript gives direct evidence of its author's relentless curiosity and his intellectual urge to understand causes and effects in nature so as to enjoy the beauty of the world through knowledge. Water is the central theme of the Codex Hammer, and of all natural phenomena it was perhaps the behaviour of water that fascinated Leonardo most consistently throughout his life. The manuscript presents Leonardo's observations on subjects ranging from astronomy to atmosphere and meteorology, and from hydraulics to canalization. These provide substantial evidence for the study of his approach to science and technology, especially his understanding of the effects produced by moving water on the earth and in the sky. In this notebook Leonardo remarked, a century before Galileo, that the secondary light of the moon (*lumen cinereum*) is sunlight reflected from the seas of the earth, and he correctly explained the presence of marine shells on mountains and plains far away from the sea, observing that 'above the plains of Italy, where flocks of birds are flying today, fishes were once moving in large shoals.' He explains an experiment with boiling water and a piston to demonstrate the motive power of steam and even digresses with a tantalising decision not to make known his invention of the submarine on account of 'the evil nature of men' who would use it treacherously to sink ships, snorkels not being so dangerous because their floating air-intake device makes them detectable.

The Codex Hammer also contributes to understanding Leonardo's art, in that the *Mona Lisa* and other late paintings offer a visual synthesis of the artist's scientific knowledge as summed up in the manuscript. The cosmological views expressed in the Codex Hammer are given visual shape in Leonardo's paintings, and the analogy which Leonardo saw between the dynamics of water and all aspects of growth and transformation in nature is expressed visually in the splendid series of water studies, including the awe-inspiring Deluge series, now in the Royal Library at Windsor.

Between 1506 and 1510, the dates suggested for the codex by comparison with others of his manuscript notebooks, Leonardo was well into his fifties and was travelling between Florence and Milan, devoting nearly all his energy to his scientific interests. The Codex Hammer is composed of 18 double-sheets or 36 folios, each written *recto* and *verso* in Leonardo's characteristic left-handed mirror script (*alla mancina*), in lines of varying length, for a total of 72 pages. The text is interspersed with approximately 360 illustrative drawings which are mainly confined to a narrow right-hand margin but which occasionally cross the page.

Leonardo's pupil Francesco Melzi inherited his master's archive on his death at Amboise in France in 1519. It is possible that the entire archive comprised upwards of ten thousand pages: much of it was reorganised by Melzi and his son Orazio and subsequently dispersed. A possible source for the Codex Hammer was a lost notebook designated by Leonardo himself as 'Libro M' in several others of his manuscripts. It is also plausible that the codex either marked the beginning of a much larger treatise on water or that it was a compendium of such a treatise. The first account of the codex dates from 1690 (a note in the State Archives in Milan) when Giuseppe Ghezzi found the notebook in a chest of manuscripts and drawings of Guglielmo della Porta and acquired it 'with the great power of gold'. Thomas Coke, later 1st Earl of Leicester (1698-1759), purchased the notebook in 1717 and brought it in about 1719 to Holkham Hall in England where it began a 261 year sojourn and was classified in the library as Holkham MS 699.

Christie's New York sale marked the second auction appearance of this particular Leonardo notebook in just fourteen years. At Christie's London, on 12 December 1980, it was sold by the Trustees of the Holkham Estate for £2,420,000 ($5,638,600). The purchaser was Dr. Armand Hammer.

The codex, untitled by Leonardo himself, was given a descriptive title by Ghezzi: *Libro Originale della natura, peso, e moto delle Acque*. The nineteenth and early twentieth-century Leonardo scholars, Jean Paul Richter and Gerolamo Calvi attached Greek-Latin sobriquets to several of the master's manuscripts for the convenience of identification and location. In the present century the manuscript became known first as Codex Leicester and has had but a brief 14-year career as Codex Hammer. On 26 July 1995 Bill Gates announced that he will re-name the manuscript Codex Leicester.

Because of its structure – 18 double sheets piled one on the other – it seems unlikely that Leonardo had the codex bound. Probably its cardboard wrapper, bearing an inscription in the hand of della Porta (d.1577), constituted its first binding. Lord Leicester had the volume rebound (a second set of central stab holes is evident) in English red morocco. With a bold flourish in 1980, Armand Hammer, guided by Dr. Carlo Pedretti, had the codex disbound to show how its pages faced each other when Leonardo compiled them. Dr. Pedretti dedicated himself to a full transcription and English translation of the text, with a compendium and photographic facsimile, which was published by Giunti Barbera of

LEONARDO DA VINCI (Italian, 1452-1519)
Autograph manuscript, titled (on an additional
eighteenth-century manuscript title-page):
'Delle Natura, Peso, e Moto delle Acque',
consisting of scientific notes and observations,
later known as Codex Leicester and
Codex Hammer (Folio 13B:24 *recto* illustrated)
72 pages (36 leaves on 18 double sheets), average
page size 11¾ x 8⅞ in. (29.9 x 22.5 cm.), written
*alla mancina* (from right to left),
in lines of varying length, interspersed with
approximately 360 illustrative drawings and
diagrams by Leonardo.
Sold by the Armand Hammer Museum of Art
and Cultural Center, Los Angeles, California.
New York, 11 November 1994,
$30,802,500 (£19,405,575)
Record auction price for a manuscript

On this page Leonardo considers obstacles affecting
currents and their use to correct anomalies in the
riverbed and to prevent damage to riverbanks.
Folio 16B:21 *recto* is illustrated as the frontispiece.

Florence in 1987. In its now unbound format the codex was widely exhibited by Dr. Hammer in nine different countries. Thus, the original manuscript, previously seen almost exclusively by a small and select group of connoisseurs, was made instantly accessible to a broad public. During all its years in England it had been publicly exhibited only on two occasions: in 1952 at the Royal Academy of Art's quincentenary exhibition commemorating Leonardo's birth, and for three days at Christie's King Street prior to its sale in 1980.

Autograph manuscripts by Leonardo da Vinci are not rare. Large concentrations are in the Biblioteca Ambrosiana in Milan, in the Royal Library at Windsor, at the British Museum and the Victoria and Albert Museum in London, at the Institut de France in Paris and the Biblioteca Nacional in Madrid. A census published in 1977 counted 33 compilations and notebooks, excluding fragments and single leaves. Their rarity in commerce, however, is demonstrated by the fact that, apart from the Codex Leicester-Hammer, no substantial manuscript has been sold since the Ashburnham dispersals towards the end of the last century. Fragmentary autograph leaves are extant in public institutions worldwide and an occasional sketch appears for sale from time to time (four small caricatures were sold at Christie's in the Chatsworth drawings sale in 1984; for another see p. 24).

It has become a cliché to refer to Leonardo as a universal genius, although undoubtedly he was precisely that. The branches of human knowledge to which he made original contributions include aerodynamics, anatomy, architecture, botany, engineering, geography, geology, hydraulics and optics; all of these in addition to painting and sculpture. Although he is regarded, together with Michelangelo, as among the greatest of Italian Renaissance artists, the body of his artistic (as opposed to scientific) work that survives is tragically small. There is no extant piece of sculpture by Leonardo; *The Battle of Anghiari*, an epic painting, was abandoned by the artist and subsequently destroyed. *The Last Supper* is a mere ghost of the original and the list of his unfinished projects is long. Only a dozen or so pictures in existence today are clearly attributable to his hand. By contrast, there are thousands of pages of his scientific writings and illustrations. The acuity of the conclusions they contain on the workings of nature often strikes us, in retrospect, as verging on the clairvoyant. Nonetheless, we know that they were arrived at and recorded by the simplest of means: observation, reflection and draughtsmanship. It is perhaps for this reason that Leonardo remains an heroic figure as much for every school child as for the great giants in the worlds of science and technology. It is a tribute to Bill Gates's tenacity as a bidder that he has succeeded in maintaining the Codex Leicester-Hammer in American ownership: even more significant, perhaps, is his public-spirited attitude in declaring his intention to share his prize on a worldwide basis through exhibitions. The codex constitutes a lot of Leonardo by any measure and Bill Gates is fortunate, indeed, to be its proud possessor.

CHARLES-AUGUSTE-JOSEPH, COMTE DE FLAHAULT
DE LA BILLARDERIE (1785-1870)
His almost complete archive, containing thousands of autograph
letters and documents by Flahault and his numerous
correspondents
Sold from the Historical Archives at Bowood House, Wiltshire
London, 12 October 1994, £111,500 ($176,170)

The illustration shows a page from an autograph letter signed by
Madame de Souza to her son Flahault, vividly describing Marshal
Ney's execution. Flahault was aide-de-camp to Napoleon and his
letters throw an important light on the Napoleonic Wars and
nineteenth-century diplomacy.

*Right:*
*Acts Passed at a Congress*
[sessions 1-3, 4 March 1789-3 March 1791]
Philadelphia and New York: Childs and Swaine, 1790-91
Folio, 12 x 7¾ in. (30.6 x 19.7 cm.)
Important Philadelphia binding of gold-tooled tree calf with
morocco lettering pieces, by James Muir. President George
Washington's copy of the complete acts of the First Congress,
containing the Constitution of the United States, Bill of Rights,
the Treaty of Paris and other fundamental legislative acts.
From the collections at Mount Vernon, of the abolitionist Senator
Joseph Roswell Hawley of Connecticut, and the pioneering
collector of American bookbindings Michael Papantonio
New York, 19 May 1995, $310,500 (£197,770)

Matthias Merian, *Le plan de la ville, cité, université et fauxbourgs de Paris* [1615]
Engraved bird's-eye plan of Paris
19½ x 39¼ in. (99.5 x 74.5 cm.)
Sold from the collection of books and views on Paris of Charles J. Liebman
New York, Christie's East, 22 February 1995,
$14,950 (£9,418)

Ian Fleming's golden Royal Quiet De Luxe typewriter, commissioned in 1952 from New York at $174, used to write all the James Bond novels starting with *Casino Royale*
11 x 11 x 6 in. (28 x 28 x 15.2 cm.)
Sold by the Hon. Mrs. Morgan, the author's stepdaughter
London, South Kensington, 5 May 1995, £55,750 ($89,869)

This gleaming but compact machine emblematises the half-fantasy world of ostentatious 1950s gadgetry so familiar from the Bond novels themselves.

FRANCIS FRITH (British, 1822-1898)
The Hypaethral Temple, Philae
from *Egypt, Sinai and Jerusalem, Photographed by Francis Frith*,
Glasgow and Edinburgh: William MacKenzie, [1860], with
twenty mammoth albumen prints each approximately
15 x 19¼ in. (37.7 x 47.9 cm.)
London, 19 October 1994, £47,700 ($78,609)

Francis Frith became particularly well-known for his
publications of photographs on Egypt, Palestine, Syria and
Nubia. He set out for Egypt in 1856 and took his
photographic van made of wicker-work with him. This
included a tent-like cloth to protect the collodion plates
from the hot climate during processing. Despite the
difficult travelling conditions and extreme heat Frith
succeeded in recording the many historic monuments of
Cairo, Thebes, Karnak, Abu Simbel and Luxor. The
photographic historian, Helmut Gernsheim describes this,
in 1955, as 'the largest book with the biggest, unenlarged
prints ever published'.

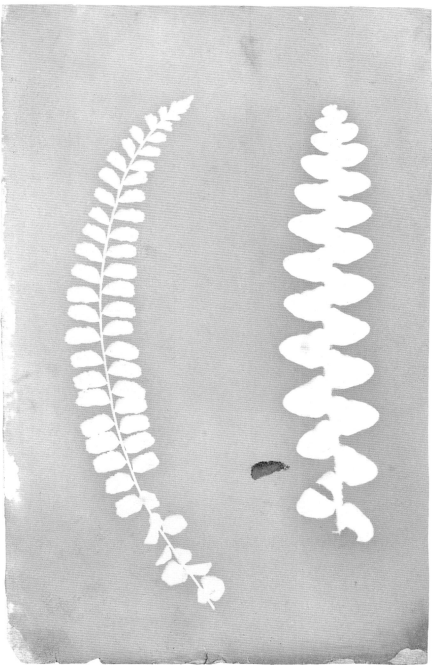

WILLIAM HENRY FOX TALBOT (British, 1800-1877)
Leaf Study
photogenic drawing negative, circa 1839
7³⁄₁₆ x 4⅜ in. (18.3 x 11.1 cm.)
Sold from the Historical Archives at Bowood House
London, 19 October 1994, £19,550 ($32,042)

The term 'photogenic drawing' was used by Talbot to
describe his first successful photographic images, made from
1834. The method was extraordinarily simple: a sheet of
plain paper was soaked in a weak salt solution, dried, and a
solution of silver nitrate applied. The object was then
placed in contact with the paper, covered and protected
by a sheet of glass and exposed to sunlight. After some time
the paper would darken leaving the image of the leaf
highlighted in negative form against the background. The
image thus formed was then fixed.

Talbot is known to have made several photographs of
botanical specimens as he prepared to announce his
invention to the public in 1839. This example was given to
Talbot's cousin, Lady Louisa Howard.

ALFRED STIEGLITZ (American, 1864-1946)
From the Back Window, 291 – N.Y., Winter – 1915
signed, titled, dated twice
platinum print, 1915
9⅜ x 7⅜ in. (22.2 x 18.5 cm.)
Sold by the family of Aline and Charles Liebman
New York, 5 April 1995, $167,500 (£104,037)

Alfred Stieglitz never tired of turning to New York's streets and skyline for inspiration. From 1902 until 1935, when he retired from photographing, he produced a series of views made from his window. This series dominates the New York photographs. Those made in the winter of 1915-16 clearly indicate his insights towards Modernism in general and Cubism in particular. However, in *From the Back Window, 291 – N.Y., Winter-1915* not only is the geometric jumble of box-like forms clearly described but the intimacy of life also shines through. The window in the lower right reveals an interior with a dinner table ready, adorned by the warmth of a three tiered candelabra.

This was not only the last Stieglitz photograph from the Liebman collection, but also the only known print of this image in private hands.

BARON ADOLPH DE MEYER
(American, 1868-1946)
For Elizabeth Arden
monogram signature in pencil in the embossed margin
gelatin silver print, circa 1940
13⅞ x 10⅞ in. (32.6 x 27.4 cm.)
Sold from the collection of Thomas Walther
New York, 5 April 1995, $140,000 (£86,957)
Record auction price for a photograph by the artist

Baron Adolph de Meyer's career was closely linked to two areas: Alfred Stieglitz and his Photo-Secessionists, and the world of fashion and editorial photography. As the first staff photographer for *Vogue*, *Vanity Fair* and, later, *Harper's Bazar* de Meyer instilled a glamour and style in fashion photography uniquely his own.

From 1927 until 1931 de Meyer created a series of advertisements for Elizabeth Arden. These involved the use of a mannequin which, through the successive advertisements, was altered and adorned with human features.

In 1940, at the age of 72, de Meyer exhibited this and other photographs in the home of his friends and patrons, Mr. and Mrs. Edward G. Robinson in Hollywood. Desperate for prints to exhibit, de Meyer had several works reprinted as enlargements but apparently producing only one of each, making this print probably unique.

# COINS

*Top, from left:*
Brunswick-Wolfenbüttel: a Friedrich Ulrich (1613-34) Glücklöser of 4-Talers, 1624
Spink, 7 March 1995, £19,800 ($32,175)
Originally sold by Spink in 1930, this splendid specimen is believed to be one of only two known.

Scotland: a James VI gold Twenty Pound Piece, 1576
Spink, 7 March 1995, £17,600 ($28,600)

Great Britain: an Oliver Cromwell Pattern Crown struck in gold, 1658, one of only two known examples
Spink, 22 November 1994, £66,000 ($103,554)

*Centre, from left:*
United States of America: a Proof Dollar, 1895
Spink America, 20 May 1995, $19,250 (£12,320)

China: a Che-Kiang Dollar, 1898-99
Spink Hong Kong, 29 November 1994, H.K.$460,000 (£38,017)

Great Britain: a George V Penny, 1933, one of only seven known examples
Spink, 22 November 1994, £25,300 ($39,696)

The Middleham Hoard
Spink, 4 July 1995, £77,275 ($123,254)

The Middleham Hoard, the largest hoard of silver coins from the Civil War ever to be discovered, contained over five thousand coins, deposited about 1647 in three pots.

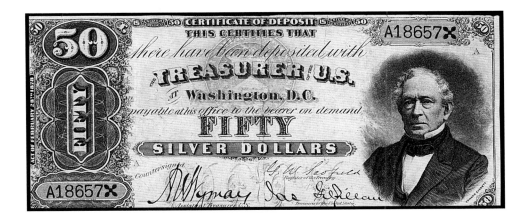

United States of America: a Fifty-Dollar
countersigned silver Certificate,
1878, serial number A18657, engraved
countersignature by A.U. Wyman
Sold from the collection of Andrew Shiva
Spink America, 22 May 1995, $46,200 (£30,900)

The 'Commando' Victoria Cross, posthumously
awarded to Lieutenant Colonel G.C.T. Keyes,
Royal Scots Greys for the 'Rommel Raid',
one of the most daring episodes of the
Second World War
Sold from the collection of Dr. Robert La Rocca
Spink, 28 March 1995, £121,000 ($193,600)

A historically important jewelled Badge of the
Order of the Iron Crown made for Napoleon by
the Imperial Jeweller, François-Regnault Nitot
1810
Spink, 28 March 1995, £44,000 ($70,400)

# STAMPS

*Above, from left:*
Hong Kong: 1882 watermark Crown CA 2c. rose variety perforation 12 printed on thick rough paper
Hong Kong, 3 May 1995, H.K.$735,000 (£58,791)

Great Britain: 1840 1d. black Plate II block of eight with Maltese Cross cancellations in red
London, 9 November 1994, £10,350 ($16,694)

Great Britain: 1910 unissued 2d. Tyrian plum
London, 14 June 1995, £11,500 ($18,331)

*Centre:*
Ceylon: 1859 4d. dull rose, two singles with 1857 1d. on cover front from Galle to London
London, 25 May 1995, £45,500 ($71,799)

Philippines: 1854 India 1a. Die II strip of four and 4a. on entire from Manila to Sydney and carried privately to Singapore
The earliest known stamped cover from the Far East
Singapore, 24 March 1995, S.$108,250 (£47,855)

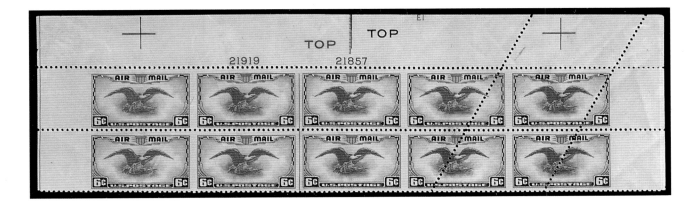

*Above:*
Hungary: 1867 3Kr. red Error of Colour, cancelled by two part strikes of the 'N.Becskerek 1/10' date stamp
Zürich, 12 April 1995, S.Fr.63,250 (£33,522)

United States: 1938 Air Mail 6c dark blue and carmine imperforate vertically a unique plate block of six in a block of ten
New York, 21 September 1994, $36,800 (£24,288)

*Centre:*
China: 1878 (c.) Elephant essay an imperforate plate proof pair in black on thick wove paper
Hong Kong, 2 November 1994, H.K.$402,500 (£31,828)

United States: 1867 15c. black E grill unused horizontal pair
New York, 21 September 1994, $27,600 (£18,216)

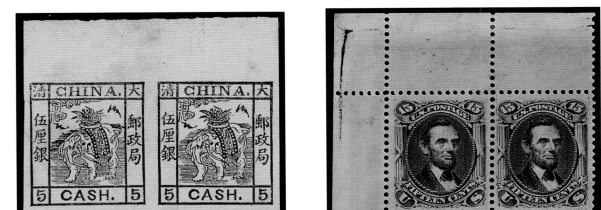

Bavaria: 1862 3Kr. greenish blue on telegram envelope
Zürich, 11 April 1995, S.Fr.9,775 (£5,181)

RAINGO FRERES (French) and LEROY ET FILS (French)
An Empire amboyna and ormolu-mounted table orrery Clock
26½ in. (67.5 cm.) high; 13¼ in. (35 cm.) diameter of base
London, 23 November 1994, £95,000 ($149,435)

HUBERT SARTON (Belgian, 1748-1828)
A Belgian ormolu and black marble complicated astronomical
world-time skeleton Clock
circa 1820
23¾ in. (60.5 cm.) high
London, 12 July 1995, £78,500 ($124,815)

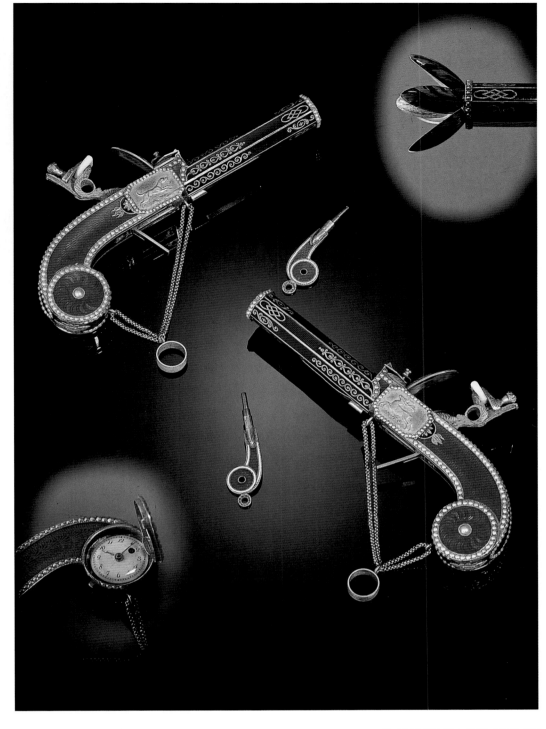

*Clockwise, from above:*
PIGUET & MEYLAN (Swiss)
A gold, enamel and pearl-set
independent dead-seconds openface
keywound cylinder Watch
signed 'P.M., No. 6537'
circa 1815
Geneva, 16 November 1994,
S.Fr.223,500 (£109,291)
Record auction price for gold, enamel
and pearl-set cylinder watch

A Pair of 18 carat gold, enamel and pearl-
set pistol-form Perfume Sprinklers with
Watches, together with matching Keys
unsigned, possibly Moulinié et Bautte
or Bautte et Moynier
circa 1810
4⅜ in. (11 cm.) long when closed
Geneva, 16 November 1994,
S.Fr.718,500 (£351,345)
Record auction price for perfume
sprinklers with watches

INTERNATIONAL WATCH CO.
A special edition *Il destriero scafusia*
perpetual calendar, minute repeating,
split second chronograph tourbillon
Wristwatch
signed 'International Watch Co'
No. 20/125
1¾ in. (4.2 cm.)
London, 23 November 1994,
£78,500 ($123,480)

CHARLES FRODSHAM
(British, 1810-1871)
A gold openface minute repeating split
second Chronograph Watch with
one-minute tourbillon
circa 1915
No. 09636
New York, 25 October 1994,
$292,622 (£178,500)

# MUSICAL INSTRUMENTS

ANTONIO STRADIVARI (Italian, 1644-1737)
A Violoncello
the back, ribs and scroll by John Lott (English, died 1871)
length of back 29½ in. (74.9 cm.)
Sold from the Estate of Janos Scholz
New York, 2 December 1994, $464,500 (£297,756)

TOMASO BALESTRIERI (Italian, active c.1750-1780)
A Violin
length of back 14¹⁄₁₆ in. (35.8 cm.)
London, 21 June 1995, £78,500 ($125,600)

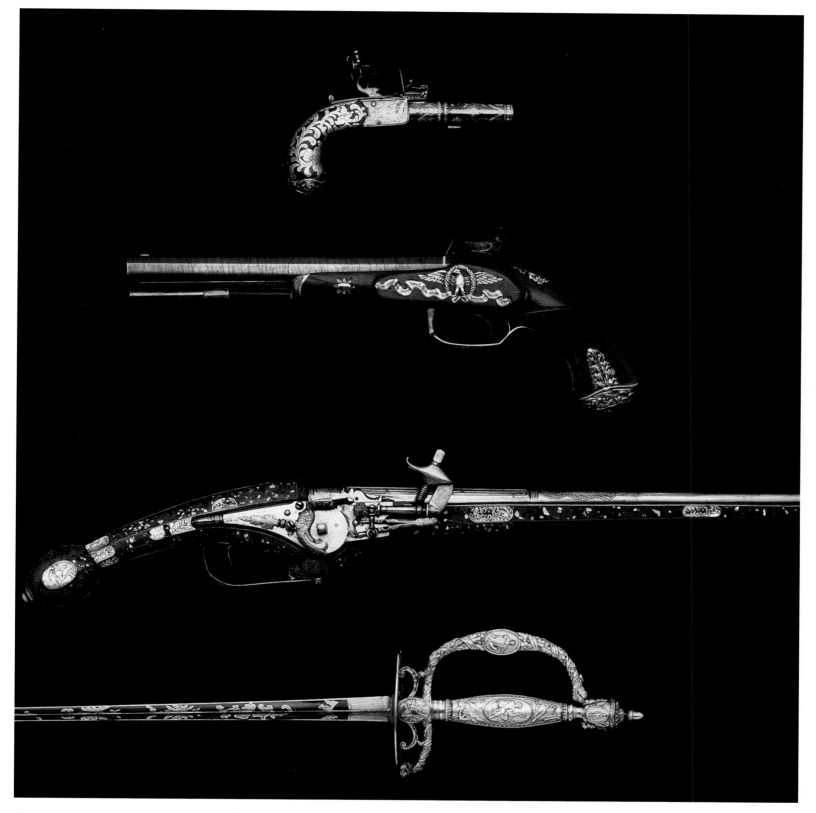

*From top:*
KNUBLEY BRUNN & CO (British, 1795-1797)
A Pair of flintlock box-lock pocket Pistols (one illustrated)
London, circa 1800, 7 in. (17.7 cm.)
London, 26 October 1994, £27,600 ($43,245)

JOHN PROSSER (British, 1796-1853)
A Pair of presentation flintlock Pistols with silver-gilt mounts
(one illustrated)
London, 1803, maker's mark 'RT', probably for Richard Teed
15½ in. (39.5 cm.)
London, 26 October 1994, £18,400 ($30,084)

A French long wheel-lock holster Pistol
early 17th Century
29½ in. (75 cm.)
London, 26 October 1994, £43,300 ($70,795)

MOSES BRENT (British, c.1750-c.1820)
A silver-gilt presentation Small-Sword, Scabbard and Case
London, 1798, 35 in. (89 cm.) blade
London, 26 October 1994, £25,300 ($41,365)

# SPORTING GUNS

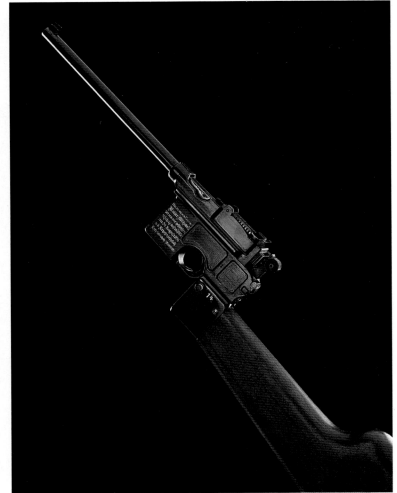

*Above, from left:*
GEORG LUGER (German)
A 7.92 mm. experimental self-loading Rifle (detail illustrated)
serial No.4
weight 9lb. 11oz.
13½ in. (34.4 cm.) pull; 27½ in. (70cm.) barrel
London, 19 July 1995, £111,500 ($177,954)

MAUSER (German)
A 7.63 mm. self-loading Carbine (detail illustrated)
serial No.1
9½ in. (24 cm.) barrel
London, 19 July 1995, £78,500 ($125,286)

JOHN RIGBY & CO. (British)
A gold-encrusted .450 (Westley Richards no. 1 case)
D.B. hammerless sidelock non-ejector Rifle (detail illustrated)
No.15673
circa 1885
weight 8lb. 9oz.; 14¾ in.(37.5 cm.) pull; 26 in. (66 cm.) barrels
Sold from the Tulchan Collection
London, 22 March 1995, £25,300 ($40,227)

A 1929 4½ Litre Bentley
Sports Tourer
Chassis No. XF3501
Engine No. XF3501
Melbourne, 28 July 1994,
A.$387,500 (£184,489)

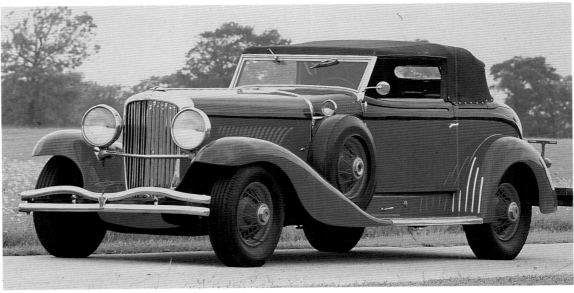

A 1933 Duesenberg Model
J Convertible Victoria
Coachwork by Rollston
Chassis No. 2535
Engine No. J-361
Body No. 532-A
Pebble Beach, 28 August 1994,
$365,500 (£215,645)

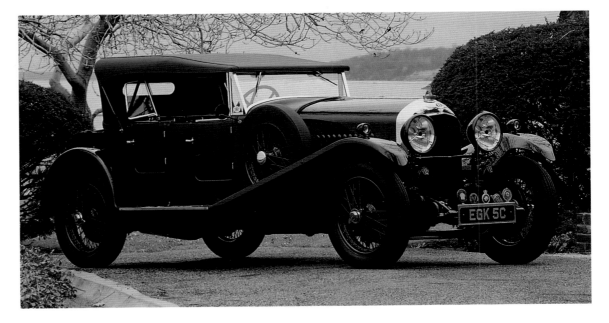

A 1929 4½ Litre Bentley
Dual Cowl Phaeton
Coachwork by Vanden Plas
Chassis No. KL3584
Engine No. KL3584
New York, 1 April 1995,
$365,500 (£225,617)

An English Court Dress or 'Mantua' of ivory silk, comprising petticoat and open robe with hooped skirts
mid 18th Century
South Kensington, 15 November 1994, £35,200 ($55,897)

A costume for *Giselle*, Act I, Prince Albrecht, 1960 Production
Sold by the Rudolf Nureyev Foundation
New York, 12 January 1995, $51,750 (£33,120)
The Nureyev sale is considered in detail in an article by
David Llewellyn on pp. 5-6.

'Teddy Girl'
A Steiff cinnamon centre seam Teddy Bear
circa 1904
18 in. (46 cm.) tall
South Kensington, 5 December 1994,
£110,000 ($171,380)
Record auction price for a teddy bear

'Teddy Girl' was the lifelong companion of the bear world's most noted collector, the late Colonel 'Bob' Henderson (1904-1990) and was given to him soon after his birth by his elder brother, Charles. Inspired by 'Teddy Girl', Colonel 'Bob' formed an extensive collection of over five hundred bears and related items. In later life, Colonel Henderson formed the British branch of the charity 'Good Bears of the World', raising money to send teddy bears to children in hospitals worldwide.

*Top, from left:*
A Dinky Toy 28 Series 'Bentalls'
Department Store Promotional Delivery Van
circa 1937
South Kensington, 14 October 1994,
£12,650 ($20,139)
Record auction price for a Dinky Toy

A Märklin tinplate Horse-Drawn Carriage
circa 1880
Carriage: 22 x 11 in. (56 x 28 cm.);
Figure: 9 in. (23 cm.) high
Christie's East, 17 November 1994,
$34,500 (£21,735)

*Above:*
A Märklin tinplate four-funnel
Ocean Liner 'Lepanto'
circa 1909
38½ in. (98 cm.)
South Kensington, 20 December 1994,
£30,800 ($48,048)

Mickey Mouse
A German lithographed tinplate Mechanical Bank,
made by Saalheimer & Strauss
early 1930s
7 in. (17.8 cm.) high
South Kensington, 24 April 1995, £15,750 ($25,467)

Charlie Parker's cream acrylic plastic Grafton alto Saxophone
early 1950s
Sold from the Chan Parker Collection
South Kensington, 8 September 1994, £93,500 ($144,364)

WALT DISNEY STUDIOS
The Plow Boy
A complete storyboard for the short featuring
Mickey and Minnie Mouse (detail illustrated)
1929, graphite and colour pencil on animation paper
12 x 9½ in. (30.5 x 24.1 cm.)
Christie's East, 9 June 1995, $101,500 (£63,636)

# *HOLLYWOOD OLD AND NEW*

## *by Nancy Cerbone Valentino*

On 28 June 1995 the saleroom at Christie's East in New York was reminiscent of an eagerly anticipated Hollywood premiere. Celebrities, television and radio personnel, spectators and serious fans all mingled together. The standing-room-only crowd had not come, however, to review a new film, but to witness the performance of classic Hollywood.

As the fever for collecting Hollywood history grows, the most desirable pieces continue to be the most iconic. The passion for vintage (1920s-1940s) film memorabilia collecting has now been joined by the current craze for contemporary (1950s-1990s) collecting. As both the 1960s and 1970s enjoy a nostalgic resurgence, Marilyn Monroe, Clark Gable and James Dean now stand alongside characters from *Batman*, *Star Trek* and *Superman*. There are certainly no finer examples of these very different, yet equally in demand collecting areas, than the car from *Casablanca*, 1943 and white suit from *Saturday Night Fever*, 1977.

The 1940 Buick Phaeton automobile was used in several Warner Bros. productions including Humphrey Bogart's *High Sierra*, 1941. However, it was the car's performance in the timeless *Casablanca* that earned it a place in the collecting hall of fame. The final heart-stopping moments of the film take place on the airport runway with Rick Blaine (Humphrey Bogart), Isla Lund (Ingrid Bergman), Victor Laszlo (Paul Henried), and Captain Louis Renault (Claude Rains). The vehicle was positioned as the central prop during Bogart and Bergman's unforgettable and tearful farewell. In addition to its memorabilia importance, the 1940 automobile has a distinct intrinsic value also. Only 230 cars of this style were ever manufactured by the American Buick car company. With 42,000 original miles, the Aztec Brown convertible features custom broadcloth interior (complete with Bogart's trademark cigarette burns), whitewall tyres and standard shift on the steering wheel.

From Rick's Cafe in Casablanca to the 2001 Odyssey Discotheque in New York, the co-star of the 28 June Film and Television sale was without a doubt, John Travolta's white three piece suit from *Saturday Night Fever*. The 1977 movie which so defined the disco decade, is still considered the standard of 1970s contemporary anthropology. John Travolta's portrayal of 'Tony Manero' as the dancing boy from Brooklyn catapulted him to stardom, while representing the frenetic and carefree decade. The suit was originally purchased by American film critic Gene Siskel for $2,000 at a 1978 charity auction, and is still one of the most recognisable costumes of all time. The film's story revolves around the night of the eagerly anticipated dance contest at the 2001 nightclub; 'Tony's' entrance onto the pulsating dance floor in the white body-hugging suit remains one of the film's most memorable moments.

Purchased by the production company at a local New York men's shop, the 100% polyester suit and black shirt, were perfectly typical of the disco era. Interestingly, the shirt and trousers were sewn together to allow Mr. Travolta the freedom to dance with ease and strike his now legendary pose.

A 1940 Buick Phaeton automobile used in *Casablanca*, 1943
Christie's East, 28 June 1995, $211,500 (£133,245)

A white Suit worn by John Travolta in *Saturday Night Fever*, 1977
Christie's East, 28 June 1995, $145,500 (£91,665)

The Maltese Falcon
Bronze patina lead Statue in the image of a Falcon
serial numer WB90066
1941
11½ in. (29 cm.) high
Sold from the collection of Mr. William Conrad
Christie's East, 6 December 1994, $398,500 (£255,040)

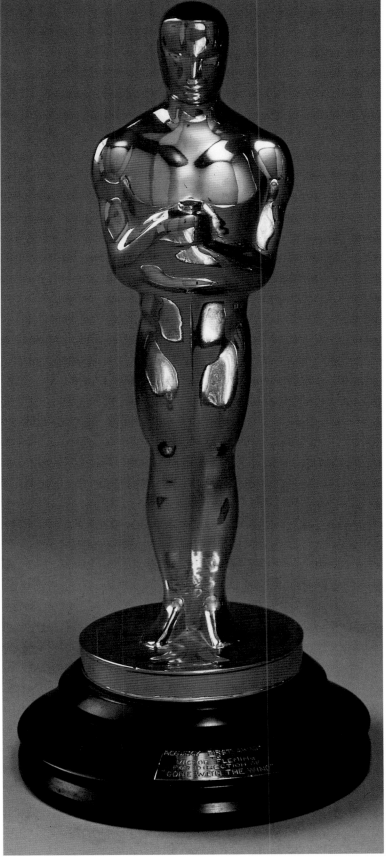

Best Director Academy Award presented to Victor Fleming
for directing *Gone With The Wind*
gold plated
1939
12 in. (30.3 cm.) high
Sold from the collection of the family of Victor Fleming
Christie's East, 6 December 1994, $244,500 (£156,480)

*Above:*
RKO
King Kong
1933, one-sheet
41 x 27 in. (104.1 x 68.6 cm.)
Christie's East, 5 December 1994, $97,100 (£63,115)

WARNER BROS.
To Have and Have Not/Acque Del Sud
1945, linen-backed, art by Luigi Martinati
79 x 55 in. (200.7 x 139.7 cm.)
South Kensington, 9 March 1995, £15,750 ($25,215)

*Right:*
Lou Gehrig's 1927 and 1928 Tour Scrapbook
Christie's East, 1 October 1994, $36,800 (£23,184)

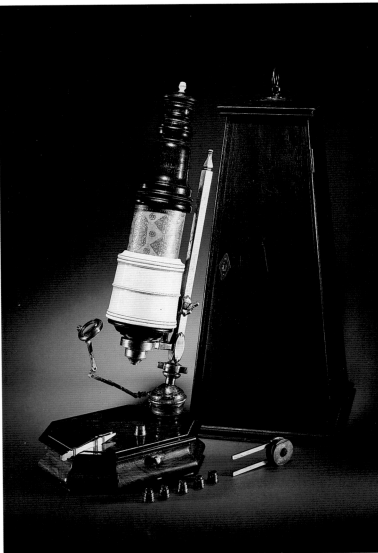

*Above, from left:*
GEORGE HARTMAN (German, 1489-1564)
A German Astrolabe
signed and dated 'GEORGIVS HARTMAN NORENBERGE
FACIEBAT ANNO 1541 MENSE IVLIO .2.'
brass, with the rete in copper
10¾ in. (27.3 cm.) diameter
South Kensington, 2 March 1995, £88,750 ($140,846)
Record auction price for an astrolabe by Hartman

JOHN and WILLIAM CARY (British)
A Pair of Library Globes (the mahogany stands attributed
to William Trotter of Edinburgh)
early 18th Century
21 in. (53.5 cm.) diameter; 48 in. (122 cm.) high
South Kensington, 6 July 1994, £70,400 ($112,217)
Record auction price for a pair of globes by Cary

*Left:*
Attributed to JOHN MARSHALL (British, 1663-1725)
A Marshall-pattern compound Monocular Microscope
18 in. (46 cm.) high
South Kensington, 29 September 1994, £30,800 ($48,356)
Record auction price for a microscope by Marshall

# WINE

## SALES IN THE UNITED KINGDOM AND OVERSEAS

*by Paul Bowker*

A full programme of forty-four sales spanning three continents and six countries reinforced both the international nature of the fine wine market and Christie's domination of it.

Sales at King Street commenced with a very Germanic flavour in two significant sales. First, on 29 September, we offered the contents of the remarkable cellar at Schloss Ramholz, family seat of Magnus von Kuhlmann, Freiherr von Stumm-Ramholz. The cellar included the most impressive range of large bottle sizes of some of the greatest wines imaginable including, remarkably, double-magnums and jéroboams (equivalent to four and six bottles respectively) of the 1893 vintage from all of the five 'first-growth' châteaux of Bordeaux. Among the most significant lots sold were an impériale (eight bottles) of Château Cheval-Blanc 1929 (£11,000) and a jéroboam (six bottles) of Château Pétrus 1945 (£15,400). The cellar sold for an astounding £397,000.

The second Germanic sale followed two weeks later on 11 October when, as part of Christie's week of German and Austrian Art, a small but high quality selection of wines from the famous Hochheim estate, Geheimrat Aschrott'sche-Erben were sold. Wines ranging from 1937 to 1993, and from Kabinett to Trockenbeerenauslese quality were offered both for tasting and for sale, and attracted considerable interest.

The holding of promotional sales for great wine-growing estates such as this has a long tradition at Christie's, with special sales having been held for most of the greatest estates of Bordeaux and elsewhere. A further such sale was held on 10 November and included representative lots from the extraordinary range of properties (ranging from Bordeaux to Portugal and Hungary) owned either by AXA-Millésimes or by the peripatetic Jean-Michel Cazes (of Château Lynch-Bages). As is always the case, the impeccable provenance of these wines, coming directly from the estate cellars, combined with their outstanding quality (as witnessed by hundreds in the largest pre-sale tasting of the season) ensured that international demand was extremely strong.

The popular evening wine auctions at Christie's South Kensington, offering more affordable wines and 'bin-ends', had an exceptionally strong season, passing the £1 million mark for the first time.

The market overall in the United Kingdom was at its strongest for over a decade, and prices for great rarities and young wines alike have reflected this. Unprecedented international demand is matched by a distinct shortage of supply for the finest wines.

Perhaps the most important event of the season was the establishment of the wine department in New York. Although Christie's have held regular and highly successful auctions in Chicago since 1981 (and indeed, Michael Broadbent was conducting auctions in the United States on behalf of Heublein as far back as 1969), wine auctions were always prohibited in New York state. This situation changed in 1994, the law being modified to allow established retailers to hold wine auctions. Christie's immediately teamed up with Zachys, the leading New York wine merchant, to prepare for an inaugural sale. The department was established in the capable hands of Ursula Hermacinski, already well-known and respected as a wine auctioneer through her strong involvement with the annual Napa Valley Wine Auctions.

The inaugural sale took place on Saturday 8 April and was one of the most spectacular and well-attended sales held by Christie's for some time, with over five hundred enthusiasts crowded into the Park Avenue salerooms. Bidding was correspondingly competitive resulting in most lots selling for prices well in excess of their estimates. Of particular note was a collection of twenty-one methusalem (eight bottle size) of wines from the seven Grand Cru vineyards of Domaine de la Romanée-Conti, belonging to baseball superstar Rusty Staub. They sold for $99,300 (£61,566) against an estimate of $60,000-80,000. An exceptionally rare bottle of Château Margaux 1900, sent for sale by the Château achieved $7,130 (£4,120), indicating once again the premium attached to provenance. The sale achieved $1,825,818 (£1,132,000) an auction record for any commercial sale of wine in the United States and the second highest total ever realised for a wine sale.

The success of the opening sale was further consolidated by the second sale in June, which also realised a total well in excess of $1 million, and the regular sales will continue to be a major feature of the auction calendar.

The regular sales in Amsterdam and Geneva both continued to show strong demand, and a relatively steady supply of top-quality wines for the bi-annual sales. The most remarkable result here was the sale in Geneva, one week after the celebration of VE Day, of a jéroboam (six bottles) of Château Mouton-Rothschild 1945, with a label celebrating 'V for Victory' for S.Fr.68,200 (£37,900), (estimate S.Fr.25,000-40,000). Auctions were also held in Tokyo (October 1994) and at Vinexpo, Bordeaux (June 1995), on the occasion of the world's largest and most important international wine fair. Total sales under the aegis of the wine department in 1994/5 rose to fractionally under £11 million, a 20% increase on the previous season.

*Top:*
Twenty-one Methusalem of Wines from the
Domaine de la Romanée-Conti (one illustrated)
Sold from the collection of Rusty Staub
New York, 8 April 1995, $99,300 (£62,024)

A complete Collection of Château Mouton-Rothschild,
1945-1991
London, 8 June 1995, £19,800 ($31,482)

*Above:*
Château d'Yquem from a German Cellar
London, 1 December 1994
1812 £13,750 ($21,532); 1825 £13,750 ($21,532);
1822 £13,750 ($21,532); 1831 £13,200 ($20,671);
1858 £8,250 ($12,919); 1847 £9,900 ($15,503)

An Impériale of Château Cheval-Blanc, 1947
London, 1 December 1994, £21,450 ($33,590)

# INDEX

# International Offices

**Isle of Man**
The Marchioness Conyngham
Myrtle Hill, Andreas Road
Ramsey, Isle of Man
Tel: (01624) 814502
Fax: (01624) 814502

**Channel Islands**
Melissa Bonn
58 David Place
St. Helier, Jersey
Tel: (01534) 877582
Fax: (01534) 877540
Richard de la Hey *Consultant*

**REPUBLIC OF IRELAND**
Desmond Fitz-Gerald
Knight of Glin, Glin Castle
Glin, Co. Limerick
Fax: (35361) 68 34 364
*Private Residence*
52 Waterloo Road, Dublin 4
Tel: (3531) 668 05 85
Fax: (3531) 668 02 71

**NORTHERN IRELAND**
Danny Kinahan
Castle Upton, Templepatrick
Co. Antrim BT39 0AH
Tel: (018494) 33480
Fax: (018494) 33410

**WORLDWIDE**

**Christie's Asia Region Office**
Philip Ng, *Managing Director, Asia*
501 Orchard Road,
# 15-02 Lane Crawford Place,
Singapore 0923
Tel: (65) 737 3884    Fax: (65) 733 7975

**SALEROOMS**

**Australia**
*Melbourne*
James B. Leslie, A.C., M.C. *Chairman*
Roger McIlroy, *Managing Director*
Christie's Australia Pty. Ltd.
1 Darling Street, South Yarra,
Victoria 3141
Tel: (613) 820 4311
Fax: (613) 820 4876

**Greece**
Elisavet Logotheti-Lyra, *Managing Director*
27 Vassilisis Sophias Avenue,
Athens 10674
Tel: (301) 725 3900
 Fax: (301) 723 8347

**Hong Kong**
Anthony Lin, *Managing Director*
Christie's Hong Kong Ltd.
2804-6 Alexandra House
16-20 Chater Road, Hong Kong
Tel: (852) 2521 5396
Telex: 72014
Fax: (852) 2845 2646

**Israel**
Mary Gilben
Christie's (Israel) Ltd
Asia House, 4 Weizmann Street
Tel Aviv 64239
Tel: (9723) 6950695
Fax: (9723) 6952751

**Italy**
*Rome*
Franz Ziegler, *Managing Director*
Francesco Alverà
Christie's (Int.) S.A., Palazzo Massimo
Lancellotti, Piazza Navona 114
Rome 00186
Tel: (396) 687 2787
 Fax: (396) 686 9902
*Florence*
Alessandra Niccolini
Di Camuglaimo
Casella Postale 62
56038 Ponsacco (PI)
Tel/Fax: (395) 877 35487

**Monaco**
Humphrey Butler (Paris)
Pascal Bégo
Christie's Monaco S.A.M.
Park Palace, 98000 Monte-Carlo
Tel: (33) 93 25 19 33
Fax: (33) 93 50 38 64

**The Netherlands**
*Amsterdam*
Charles André de la Porte, *Chairman*
Victor J. E. Moussault, *Managing Director*
Christie's Amsterdam B.V.
Cornelis Schuytstraat 57
1071 JG Amsterdam
Tel: (3120) 57 55 255
Fax: (3120) 66 40 899
*Rotterdam*
Coolsingel 93, P.O. Box 21320
3001 AH Rotterdam
Tel: (3110) 414 3202
Fax: (3110) 412 6896

**Singapore**
Irene Lee
Cecilia Ong, *Consultant*
Christie's International Singapore Pte Ltd.
Unit 3, Parklane
Goodwood Park Hotel,
22 Scotts Road, Singapore 0922
Tel: (65) 235 3828    Fax: (65) 235 8128

**Switzerland**
François Curiel, *President*
Guy Jennings, *Vice President*
Christie's (Int.) S.A.
8 Place de la Taconnerie
1204 Geneva
Tel: (4122) 311 1766
Fax: (4122) 311 5559

**Taiwan**
Anthony Lin, *Managing Director*
Diana Kang, Carol Huang
Christie's Hong Kong Ltd, Taiwan Branch
6th Floor, 369 Fu-Hsing North Road
Taipei 10483, Taiwan, R.O.C.
Tel: (8862) 718 1612
Fax: (8862) 718 3702

**REPRESENTATIVES**

**Australia**
*Sydney*
Janelle Dawes
298 New South Head Road
Double Bay, Sydney, N.S.W. 2028
Tel: (612) 326 1422    Telex: 26343
Fax: (612) 327 8439
*Adelaide*
Ian Bruce
446 Pulteney Street, Adelaide S.A. 5000
Tel: (618) 232 2860    Fax: (618) 232 6506
*Brisbane*
Michael Reid
482 Brunswick Street, Fortitude Valley
Brisbane 4006, Queensland
Tel: (617) 254 1499    Fax: (617) 254 1566

**Austria**
Dr. Johanna Schönburg-Hartenstein
Christie's Kunstauktionen GmbH
Kohlmarkt 4, 1010 Vienna
Tel: (431) 533 88 12
Fax: (431) 533 71 66

**Belgium**
Bernard de Launoit, *General Manager*
Sabine Taevernier, *Contemporary Art*
Roland de Lathuy, *Old Master Pictures*
Bernard Steyaert, *Chairman*
Christie's Belgium S.A.
33 Boulevard de Waterloo, 1000 Brussels
Tel: (322) 512 8830
Fax: (322) 513 3279

**People's Republic of China**
Lillian Chu
Christie's Shanghai Ltd
Suite 404, American International Centre
1376 Nanjing Road West,
Shanghai 200040
Tel: (8621) 279 8773
Fax: (8621) 279 8771

**Denmark**
Birgitta Hillingsø
Dronningens Tværgade 10
1302 Copenhagen K
Tel: (45) 33 32 70 75
Fax: (45) 33 13 00 75

**Finland**
Barbro Schauman
Ulrikagatan 3 A, 00140 Helsinki
Tel: (3580) 60 82 12
Fax: (3580) 66 06 87

**France**
*Paris*
Nicholas Clive Worms, *Chairman*
Humphrey Butler, *Managing Director*
Hugues Joffre, *Deputy Chairman*
Bertrand du Vignaud, *Deputy Chairman*
Jean-René Saillard, *General Manager*
Christie's France S.A.
6 rue Paul Baudry, 75008 Paris
Tel: (331) 42 56 17 66
Fax: (331) 42 56 26 01
*Aix-en-Provence*
Fabienne Albertini
28 rue Lieutand
13100 Aix en Provence
Tel: (33) 92 72 43 31   Fax: (33) 92 72 53 65
*Bordeaux*
Marie-Cecile Moueix
49 Cours Xavier Arnozan, 33000
Bordeaux
Tel: (33) 56 81 65 47    Fax: (33) 56 51 15
71
*Lyon*
Vicomte Thierry de Lachaise
36 Place Bellecourt, 69002 Lyon
Tel: (33) 78 42 83 82  Fax: (33) 78 42 83 84

**Germany**
*Düsseldorf*
Jörg-Michael Bertz, *Deputy Chairman*
Birgid Seynsche-Vautz, *Administration Manager*
Christie's (Deutschland) GmbH
P.O. Box 101810 Inselstrasse 15
40479 Düsseldorf
Tel: (49211) 498 2986
Fax: (49211) 492 0339
*Berlin*
Marianne Kewenig
Andrea Fiuczynski *Director European Furniture*
Viktoria von Specht
Barbara Bergdolt
Fasanenstrasse 72, 10719 Berlin
Tel: (4930) 882 7778    Fax: (4930) 883 8768
*Frankfurt*
Charlotte Prinzessin von Croÿ
Julia Pfeffer
Arndtstrasse 18
60325 Frankfurt am Main
Tel: (4969) 74 50 21    Fax: (4969) 75 20 79
*Hamburg*
Christiane Gräfin zu Rantzau
Wentzelstrasse 21, 22301 Hamburg
Tel: (4940) 279 4073    Fax: (4940) 270 4497
*Munich*
Marie Christine Gräfin Huyn
Residenzstrasse 27, 80333 Munich
Tel: (4989) 22 95 39   Fax: (4989) 29 63 02

**Greece**
Christie's Thessalouiki
Aristotelous 8
546 23 Thessalaniki
Tel: (3031) 244 607    Fax: (3031) 242 931

**India**
Amrita Jhaveri
Christie's Bombay
26 Ridge Road, Malabar Hill
Bombay 400-006
Tel: (9122) 363 3415
Fax: (9122) 363 3629

**Italy**
*Milan*
Clarice Pecori Giraldi, Tito Pedrini
Christie's (Int.) S.A.
Via Manin 3, 20121 Milan
Tel: (392) 29 00 13 74
Fax: (392) 29 00 11 56
*Turin*
Sandro Perrone di San Martino
Corso Matteotti 33, 10121 Turin
Tel: (3911) 548 819    Fax: (3911) 542 710
*Padova*
Contessa Isabelle von Schoenfeldt
Palazzo Buzzaccarini
Via Eugenea 23, 35100 Padova
Tel: (39) 49 871 9651
Fax: (39) 49 871 9424
*Bologna*
Franco Calarota
Via M. D'Azeglio 15, 40123 Bologna
Tel: (3951) 235 843   Fax: (3951) 222 716

*Genoa*
Rachele Giucciardi
Via Belvedere Montaldo 5, 16122 Genoa
Tel: (3910) 247 1204

**Japan**
Sachiko Hibiya, *Deputy Chairman*
Koji Yamada, *Managing Director*
Christie's Japan Ltd.
Sankyo Ginza Blg, 6-5-13 Ginza
Chuo-ku, Tokyo 104
Tel: (813) 3571 0668
Fax: (813) 3571 5853

**Luxembourg**
Countess Marina von Kamarowsky
16 Wurth-Paquet
2737 Luxembourg
Tel: (352) 44 04 95    Fax: (352) 44 04 92

**Norway**
Ulla Solitair Hjort
Christie's
Colbjornsensgt, 1, 0256 Oslo 2
Tel: (4722) 44 12 42
Fax: (4722) 55 92 36

**Portugal**
Mafalda Pereira Coutinho
Rua da Lapa, 67
1200 Lisbon
Tel: (3511) 396 9750
Fax: (3511) 396 9732

**Singapore**
Asia Regional Office
Philip Ng, *Managing Director, Asia*
501 Orchard Road,
15-02 Lane Crawford Place
Singapore 0923
Tel: (65) 737 3884  Fax: (65) 733 7975

**South Korea**
Heakyum Kim, Suite #1212,
Shilla Hotel, 202, 2Ga, Jang Chung-Dong
Chang-Ku, Seoul
Tel: (822) 230 3760    Fax: (822) 230 3768

**South Africa**
*Cape Town*
Juliet Lomberg
14 Hillwood Road
Claremont, Cape Town 7700
Tel: (2721) 761 2676    Fax: (2721) 762 7129
*Johannesburg*
Harriet Hedley
P.O. Box 72126, Parkview
Johannesburg 2122
Tel: (2711) 486 0967
Fax: (2711) 646 0390

**Spain**
Casilda Fz-Villaverde y Silva
Juan Varez
Christie's Iberica S.L.
Antonio Maura 10, 28014 Madrid
Tel: (341) 532 66 26/7
Fax: (341) 523 12 40

**Sweden**
*Stockholm*
Lillemor Malmström
Sturegatan 26, 11436 Stockholm
Tel: (468) 662 0131
Fax: (468) 660 0725
*South of Sweden*
Baroness Irma Silfverschiold
230 41 Klagerup
Tel: (4640) 44 03 60
Fax: (4640) 44 03 71

**Switzerland**
*Lugano*
Marchesa Cornelia Pallavicini
Via Soave, 9
6900 Lugano Switzerland
Tel: (4191) 922 2031
Fax: (4191) 922 2032
*Zürich*
Maria Reinshagen, *Vice President*
Catherine Reymond, *Administration Manager*
Stefan Puttaert-Spiess
*(Professional Advisers)*
Christie's (Int.) A.G.
Steinwiesplatz, 8032 Zürich
Tel: (411) 2681010
Fax: (411) 2681011

6/1/99